Theogony
Works and Days

Theogony
Works and Days

HESIOD

Translated by
C.S. Morrissey

*With a foreword by Roger Scruton
and an afterword by Eric Voegelin*

Talonbooks

Translation copyright © 2012 C.S. Morrissey

Talonbooks
9259 Shaughnessy Street,
Vancouver, B.C.
V6P 6R4

www.talonbooks.com

Typeset in Minion and printed and bound in United States.

Cover illustration by Daniel Mackie
Cover design by Typesmith

Third printing: 2021

The publisher gratefully acknowledges the financial support of the Canada
Council for the Arts, the Government of Canada through the Canada Book
Fund and the Province of British Columbia through the British Columbia
Arts Council and the Book Publishing Tax Credit for our publishing activities.

Library and Archives Canada Cataloguing in Publication

Hesiod
    Theogony ; Works and days / Hesiod ; translated by C.S. Morrissey ; with
a foreword by Roger Scruton ; and an afterword by Eric Voegelin.

Translation of: Theogonia and Erga kai Hemerai.
Translated from the Ancient Greek.
Also issued in electronic format.
ISBN 978-0-88922-700-2

    1. Hesiod—Translations into English. 2. Religious poetry,
Greek—Translations into English. 3. Didactic poetry, Greek—Translations
into English. I. Morrissey, C. S. (Christopher Stewart), 1967– II. Title.
III. Hesiod. Works and days. English. IV. Hesiod. Theogony. English.

PA4010.E5T5 2012   881'.01   C2012-903996-9

To the philomythoi

– those people from whom
I have received
the most,
especially my wife, Angela

... the two Hesiodic compositions
can be understood synchronically
as two halves
of an organic whole,
a diptych, as it were,
in which each component
illuminates the other.

– JENNY STRAUSS CLAY,
  Hesiod's Cosmos

Contents

PART HUMAN: Hesiod's *Works*

Acknowledgments

Thanks to the students who took my Introduction to Classical Mythology course in the spring 2011 semester at Simon Fraser University, Harbour Centre. Our classroom conversations stimulated me to arrive at a fresh appreciation and interpretation of Hesiod's poetry, beginning with a new *Theogony* translation. Thanks also to Garry Thomas Morse for encouraging me to finish the project with a fresh rendition of the *Works and Days*. I am grateful to him and to Talonbooks for bringing into print this loving tribute to Hesiod and the Muses. Many thanks to Greg Gibson for his careful editorial attention to each line of the manuscript and for helping me with many improvements.

Foreword

To translate a foundational text is to expose yourself, your world, and your historical moment to an undying vision. Of Hesiod is this especially true. He looks down on us with the eyes of his gods, prising open our secrets, showing the flawed contours of the human soul without the social and cultural embellishments that have enabled us to hide them. There is, in his verses, a divine simplicity that carries complete conviction. And, when we recognize ourselves in his accounts of the rugged life that he knew, we acknowledge that we too need the *nomos*; we too depend upon custom and upon the natural and eternal justice without which we cannot live in peace with our neighbors or build a world that we share.

C.S. Morrissey places a very modern sensibility under the light of these precious verses, and his translations remind us at every point that Hesiod's gods are still with us, not as subjects to be worshipped and appeased through sacrifice, but as enduring motives that govern and disrupt our lives.

ROGER SCRUTON
Scrutopia, January 2012

Translator's Note

This translation aims to present Hesiod's poetry as engaging storytelling, unmediated by distracting footnotes and scholarly nitpicking. The Greek is translated accurately, if at times expansively – nevertheless, every expansive interpretation is rooted in the Greek text. In my original manuscript, each line of Greek source text corresponded directly to a single line in English translation. Any expansions in the English never went more than one line beyond where they originated in correspondence to the Greek. On rare occasions, words from one line appeared in the immediately previous or immediately following line, if it was necessary in order to achieve more natural English syntax within the sentence. Reformatted for publication, the one-to-one line correspondence in my original manuscript has been broken up so that the translation of each Greek line is now spread over two (and usually only two) lines of English. This format allows for plenty of white space on the page and is intended to provide a more pleasant experience for the reader.

Words not found in the Greek text have sometimes been added to the translation as explanatory information for English readers unfamiliar with Greek mythology. The inclusion of this information thereby saves these readers from the drudgery of referring to footnotes. The rule I have followed in this regard is that explanatory additions to the text do not exceed the length of the one English line to which they are inserted when expanding upon the thought in the one Greek line. Information that Hesiod assumed his Greek listener already knew has occasionally been added, without scruple, to this translation. Again, this is done for the ease and pleasure thereby granted the reader. Because it is often cumbersome to refer back and forth to a glossary, both English and Greek versions of names are frequently given side by side in the text for the reader's convenience. When I felt it appropriate to do so, I have flagged the appearance of a significant divinity's or individual's name with italics. Think of it as an increase in brightness as someone enters briefly into the spotlight. Transliterated Greek words are also set in italics. I use a mix of Greek and Roman spellings in English translation for aesthetic reasons. Often the familiar Roman version of a name seemed best for a reader.

The chapter divisions, titles, and subheadings are all additions of my own invention. They aim to make the storytelling as accessible as possible. They also highlight some hitherto unnoticed parallel symmetries constructed around the central Prometheus episode of *Theogony*, Chapter 5. For example, the careful reader will see the parallels between Chapters 4 and 6, between Chapters 3 and 7, between Chapters 2 and 8, and between Chapters 1 and 9. It is confidently assumed that Hesiod would approve of these chapter divisions, especially since, nine in number, they honor the Muses.

I have consulted the texts of West (1966, 1978), the translations of Lattimore (1959), Frazer (1983), Athanassakis (1983), Caldwell (1987), Grene (1998), and the Loeb editions of Evelyn-White (1914) and Most (2006). But any scholarly disputes that the translation simply settles without comment, and any innovative interpretations of Hesiod's story that shine forth in this translation's modern storytelling, are unapologetically offered here to the reader as the humble obedience of the translator to the Muses' divine instruction. Still, blame me for any clunkers, and never them.

I have chosen to render the important Greek word *thumos* as "competitive spirit" (instead of either "anger" or "spirit"). This may seem like I am giving Hesiod lessons in the anthropology of René Girard, but the insights gained by this simple maneuver, which unlock a key theme in Hesiod's poetry, are worth the price of any knee-jerk skeptical jeers. This translation choice also allows the *Theogony* to sound out themes taken up more explicitly in the *Works*. It thus highlights the frequently unappreciated unity of Hesiod's speculative reflections about human experience. I believe these reflections foreshadow, if not inspire, Plato's analysis of *thumos*, that highly ambiguous structure within the human soul.

There are some instances where I can be accused of using anachronistic images (for example, "laxatives" and "toilet paper"), but I am unapologetic about these, because on extraordinary and important occasions a translator simply must translate what he thinks the poet means and not what he says. On such occasions I have left myself open to criticism for making interpolations. But as with Christopher Logue's refreshing renderings of Homer, I hope my acts of imagination will provide reading pleasure and thereby their own justification. Pedants will pull faces, but I am a deliberately unconventional translator, in pursuit of goals higher than their fettered imaginations and professional resentments.

The ingenuity of the Muses bestows holy gifts: always just the right number of words for something wondrous, given gratuitously. Hesiod has heard their voice. No translation can ever match his divine verses. I seek only to pay tribute to his memory and to suggest something of the joy to be found by drawing near, however we are able, in all humility, to the source of his inspiration.

CHRISTOPHER S. MORRISSEY
Langley, British Columbia

Hesiod's *Theogony*

The Sacred Dance

Let us begin,
singing of the *Muses* of Helicon.
The great sacred mountain, Helicon,
belongs to them.
Around its deep-blue spring,
with gentle feet
they shall dance, worshipping
at the altar of *Zeus*, the mighty son of Cronus.
First they bathe their soft skin
in the stream Permessus, or in the Hippocrene   5
(the Spring of the Horse) sprung by Pegasus' hoof,
or in the sacred river Olmeius.
Then up on the peak of Helicon,
they put their feet into the dance.
They are beautiful.
With passion and grace, they move nimbly.

The Sacred Hymns

They rise up in excitement, high on the peak.
Under abundant mist,
in the middle of the night,
they chant the most beautiful music.   10
They hymn to *Zeus*, him who holds the aegis,
and to her, Queen *Hera*, the Argive
who walks in golden sandals,
and to the daughter of Zeus the aegis holder,
steely-eyed *Athena*,
and to shining *Apollo*,
and to *Artemis*, the archeress,
and to *Poseidon*, Earth Holder and Earth Shaker,   15
and to compassionate *Themis*,
and to *Aphrodite* with the darting eyes,

and to golden-crowned *Hebe*,
and to beautiful *Dione*,
to *Leto* and *Iapetus* and *Cronus*
(he of the famously evil stratagem),
to Dawn (*Eos*) and great Sun (*Helius*)
and shining Moon (*Selene*),
to Earth (*Gaia*) and great Ocean (*Oceanus*)
and black Night (*Nyx*),   20
to the others of the sacred family of immortals,
they who live forever.

Hesiod's Inspiration

The Muses once taught Hesiod
a song, a beautiful song.
He was shepherding sheep
by sacred Helicon.
And this is the very first thing
the goddesses said to me. This is a direct quote
from the Muses of Olympian Zeus,
from the daughters of the aegis holder: 25
"Shepherds are bumpkins. They are a disgrace.
They think of nothing but the next meal.
We, we know how, with lies, to tell a tale.
Lies that, in so many ways, resemble the truth.
We, we know how, when we wish,
even to sing flat-out about what is real."

So said the clear-speaking daughters
of great Zeus.
Then they gave me the staff of authority,
a branch of luxuriant laurel   30
they had plucked, wondrous to behold.
They breathed into me a voice
inspired, so I might celebrate
what will be and what has been.
They bid me to hymn the family
of the blessed, they who live forever.
They of the same, from first to last,

always sing.
And what have these things (more to sing)
to do with oak or rock, with what is real?   35

The Holy Family

You are blessed, so let us begin
with you, *O Muses*. You, to your father, Zeus,
sing hymns, delighting him,
the great mind of Olympus.
You say what is and what
will be and what has been.
Harmonious are your voices.
Sound flows effortlessly,
sweetly from your mouths.
A father's roar of delight fills the palaces of   40
Zeus (he who makes loud sounds) when
your delicate song, like a lily,
starts to spread itself out. It peals
across the peaks of snowy Olympus and
throughout the palaces of the immortals.
You send your divine melodies
in celebration of the revered
family of the gods. You start
from the beginning, when from Earth (*Gaia*)
and wide Sky (*Uranus*) they were born,   45
they, the Titans, from whom the Olympian gods,
who now give blessings to us, came.
Finally, you celebrate Zeus,
the Zeusfather of gods and husbands.
It is he for whom you Muses begin
your hymns and end your songs.
You celebrate how he surpasses
all the gods, in power and might.
Along the way, you tell the story
of the family of humans, and of the powerful Giants,   50
and in so doing you delight Zeus,
the mind of Olympus.

The Story of the Muses; or, Nine Carefree Nights

You, O Muses of Olympus, are
the daughters of Zeus, who holds the aegis.
In Pieria, she lay with your father,
Zeus, and she gave birth,
she, your mother, Memory (*Mnemosyne*).
Guarding the fields of Freedom (*Eleuther*),
she lay with him to forget her troubles
and to take a break from all her cares.   55
For nine nights, strategic Zeus
(he made good use of his time) lay with her,
far away from the immortals.
In the sacred bed, he made his ascent.
But then the year went on.
The seasons turned, around
the passing months. A length of days
was completed.
She gave birth to nine daughters. Like her in mind,
only for the song in their hearts   60
do they care. They do not carry
a competitive spirit weighted with cares.

Praise for a Lawful King

Down a little from the highest
summit of snowcapped Olympus,
the Muses' radiant choirs and beautiful palaces
are there.
Beside them the Graces (*Charites*)
and Sweet Longing (*Himerus*) dwell also,
ready for the festival. Lovely is the sound
sent forth from their mouth.   65
In song and dance they celebrate
the laws and customs cherished by all
the immortals. In praise,
they chant out, lovely.
Then they go up Olympus,
exulting in their beautiful voice

and divine dance. All around them,
the dark Earth resounds
as they hymn. A charming beat
rises up from beneath their feet   70
as they move towards their father.
He is King over the Sky.
He it is who holds the thunder
and the smoldering bolt.
He conquered his father, Cronus,
with that power. Then justly with each of
the immortals did he establish right order for all.
He guarded their honors.
Of these things (more indeed to sing), the Muses,
who hold palaces on Olympus, now do sing.   75

The Real Gift of Kings

Nine daughters, the Muses are
the offspring of great Zeus:
Cleio and *Euterpe* and
Thaleia and *Melpomene* and
Terpsichore and *Erato* and
Polyhymnia and *Urania* and
Calliope, who is the most
excellent of them all,
for it is she who attends
to revered kings the most.   80
Whichever king the daughters of great Zeus
attend to with reverence,
whichever king they watch from
birth (since all kings are raised up by Zeus),
it is upon his tongue they pour
a sweet dew, so that
from his mouth gentle words
might flow. The people
all look to him. He comes
to decisions about the laws   85
with frank judgments.
He addresses them steadfastly,

to quickly and skillfully end
even a great quarrel.
Kings are prudent. The need is clear.
The need for people
who harm one another is
an end to it.
In the Assembly there is an end to vengeful deeds.
Retaliation appears easily. But he talks things
over, persuades with soft words.   90
As he walks into the Assembly, they seek,
as if he were a god, to win his favor
with gracious deference.
Among those assembled, he is conspicuous.
Such is the Muses' sacred gift
for humans.
Thanks to the Muses
and far-shooting Apollo,
men on the ground
can be poets and musicians.   95
But a king? He is from Zeus. And fortunate is he,
the king whom the Muses also
love. A sweet voice streams
from his mouth.

Poets Resemble Good Kings

If anyone is suffering,
from a freshly wounded competitive spirit,
if anyone has a heart
dried out by sorrows, the poet,
servant of the Muses,
sings of the deeds of past humans   100
in a hymn. In this hymn, he sings
of the blessed gods who hold Olympus.
At once anxieties are forgotten.
Not a single worry
is recalled. Quickly do they divert, they,
the gifts of the goddesses, the gifts of the Muses.

The Story of the Gods

Welcome, children of Zeus.
Grant to me your charming song.
Praise the holy family of immortals,
who live forever.   105
Celebrate those born from the Earth (*Gaia*)
and the Sky (*Uranus*), sparkled with stars.
Celebrate those to whom dark Night (*Nyx*)
and salty Sea (*Pontus*) gave birth.
Tell us how the first gods
came into being, the Earth and
the rivers and the never-ending Sea,
its raging surge, and
the shining stars and
wide Sky above. Tell us how   110
the Olympian gods, who now
give blessings to us,
shared the abundance and
allocated honors. Tell us
when it was they first came to possess
Mount Olympus, with its manifold valleys.

O Muses, who hold palaces on Olympus,
say to me these things (the more to sing).
Speak to me, from the beginning:
who came first?   115

CHAPTER 1: *Castration*
(The Succession Myth, Part 1)

The First

First of all, *Chaos* (the Void)
came spontaneously into being. But then came
the broad-breasted Earth (*Gaia*).
She is ever the steadfast abode for those
immortals who live on the peak
of snowcapped Olympus.
Then came dark *Tartarus* (the Underworld)
underneath the ground's wide path.
Then came *Eros* (Desire), who is
the most beautiful of the immortal gods.   120
She loosens limbs.
For all gods, for all humans,
heartfelt Desire subdues
even earnest intent and careful deliberation.

Descendants of the Void; or, The Next

Darkness (*Erebos*) and black Night (*Nyx*)
came spontaneously into being, from the Void.
Then, in turn, from Night came
Brightness (*Aether*) and Day (*Hemera*). But
Night gave birth to them after conceiving them
in sexual intercourse with Darkness.   125

The Three Children of the Earth

First, Earth (*Gaia*) brought forth
her perfect match,
Sky (*Uranus*), sparkled with stars.
He would shelter her everywhere.
She would be the steadfast abode

for the blessed gods always.
Then, she brought forth the large Mountains (*Ourea*),
the lovely haunts of goddesses.
Indeed, Nymphs dwell throughout
the wooded mountains.   130
Then, she gave birth to
the unplowed expanse, the raging surge,
the Sea (*Pontus*). All this she did
without sexual intercourse. But then …

The Eighteen Children of Earth and Sky

Earth lay with Sky. She gave birth
to deep-eddying Ocean (*Oceanus*)
and *Coeus* and *Crius*
and *Hyperion* and *Iapetus*
and *Theia* and *Rhea*
and *Themis* and *Mnemosyne*   135
and golden-crowned *Phoebe*
and charming *Tethys*.
After these, she brought forth her youngest,
Cronus, he of the famously evil stratagem.
Of all the children, he was the most formidable.
For his lusty father, he conceived hatred.

Then, she brought forth
the Cyclopes, lawless at heart.
Brontes and *Steropes* and *Arges*
were mightily competitive in spirit.   140
It was they who later gave thunder to Zeus.
The thunderbolt was originally theirs.
They resembled the gods
in most respects. But
they had only one eye. It lay in
the middle of their foreheads.
They were called
the "Round-Eyed Ones" (*Cyclopes*) because of
the one round eye
on their foreheads.   145

Strength, force, and wiliness
characterize their deeds.

Then, still more came
from Earth and Sky.
Three large, mighty children,
the infamously abominable
Cottus and *Briareus* and *Gyges*,
were the most insolent of offspring.
One hundred hands and arms
shot out from their shoulders   150
(befitting their greedy nature), and
fifty heads for each
grew from the fifty shoulders
of the hundred-strong limbs.
Strength, monstrosity, might:
such was their overwhelming appearance.

The Castration of the Sky

In fact, all who came forth
from Earth and Sky were
the most formidable of children.
They conceived hatred for their father   155
from the moment of conception.
Whenever any one of them first began to exist,
he would keep them stuffed inside,
each and every one. None could exit and see the light
outside Earth's dark hole. By this evil deed,
he was able to keep on taking his pleasure,
he, insatiable Sky. The gigantic Earth
began to groan. Congested inside,
she felt the strain. So she devised
a gambit both evil and skillful.   160
With haste, mining her stock
of adamantine steel,
she built a massive sickle,
and displayed it to her children.

Exhorting them, she spoke,
but with sorrow in her dear heart:

"My children, your father is wicked.
If you have the will,
then obey me. We must pay back
the evil disgrace of the father,   165
your father, because he was the first
to resolve to do disgraceful deeds."

So said she. But fear seized them all.
Not one of them
made a sound. Suddenly great Cronus
(he of the famously evil stratagem) became bold.
In reply, he addressed his noble mother
with these words:

"Mother, I at least
promise to do this and to complete   170
the deed, since I at least take no heed
of the hateful father,
our father, because he was the first
to resolve to do disgraceful deeds."

So said he. And gigantic Earth
greatly rejoiced in spirit.
She placed him under cover,
in ambush. She placed in his hands
the sharp-toothed sickle. She suggested to him
the entire gambit.   175

Then great Sky came, bringing on
the Night. Embracing the Earth,
he pressed upon her, desiring intercourse.
Alongside her, he laid out
fully extended. Then, from the place of
ambush, his son stretched out his hand
on the left. With his right hand,
he took hold of the massive sickle,
long and sharp-toothed.

The genitals of his own dear father   180
he furiously mowed down.
He sent them flying, throwing them away
behind his back. But they did not escape
from his hand to no purpose.
Every bit of blood
that sprayed out,
the Earth received all of it.
As the years wound by, from it
she brought forth the powerful Furies (*Erinyes*),
and the great Giants (*Gigantes*).   185
In their armor, they were radiant.
In their hands, they were holding long spears.
Then, all over the boundless Earth, came forth
the nymphs called the Ash-Tree Nymphs.

The Birth of Aphrodite; or, The Comeback

Right when Cronus, with adamantine blade,
severed the Sky's genitals,
he cast them from the mainland
into the wave-washed Sea.
For a long time, they were carried over
its expanse. Then suddenly a white   190
foam broke forth on the surface
of the immortal skin. In it, a young girl
grew up.
First, to sacred Cythera
she made her approach. Then she reached
Cyprus next, a place surrounded by water.
When the goddess, tender beauty, set foot
on the land, around her the meadow green
flowered beneath
the tread of her slim feet. "Aphrodite,   195
the goddess at home in the foam";
"Cytherea, crowned with flowers":
that's what gods and men call her,
because in the foam
she grew up. But they call her Cytherea

because she surfed ashore at Cythera.
Also, "Cyprus-Born" (*Cyprogenes*),
because she came forth in wave-washed Cyprus.
Also, "Miss Congenitalia" (*Philommeides*),
because she appears genial about genitals (*medea*).   200

Desire (*Eros*) accompanied her,
and beautiful Sweet Longing (*Himerus*) attended her,
right from her time of birth,
when she entered the clan of the gods.
Ever since she began, she has held
this honor. She has been put in possession of
this destiny among humans
and the immortal gods:
the whispers, smiles,
and deceptions   205
of a young girl – her sweet
delight, affection, and gentle charm.

Titanic Grit

It was from their father that they received
the name Titans, meaning "Grits" (*Titanes*).
Great father Sky had abused these
children whom he himself sired.
But he said that they "showed grit and determination"
(*titainontes*) to perform the wildly
great deed. Yet there will be, for such a deed,
unavoidable retribution, coming soon.   210

CHAPTER 2: *A Night of Monsters*
(Aphrodite's Flood of Genealogy Begins)

A Chaotic Night of Retribution;
or, The Grandchildren of the Void

Night (*Nyx*) bore hateful Doom (*Moros*)
and black Destiny (*Ker*)
and Death (*Thanatos*). Night bore Sleep (*Hypnos*)
and the tribe of Dreams (*Oneiroi*).
Then, Night bore Blame (*Momus*)
and painful Misery (*Oizys*).
But black Night had not lain with
any of the gods. Still, she bore
the Daughters of Evening (*Hesperides*),
who beyond famous Ocean there   215
tend to the beautiful golden apples
and to the trees bearing that fruit.
She also brought forth the Fates (*Moirai*)
and Destinies (*Keres*), who pitilessly punish:
Clotho (Spinner of Life's Thread), *Lachesis*
(Dispenser of Lots), and *Atropos* (Not for Turning).
As mortals are born, they give to them
the good and evil they will have.
They pursue the transgressions
of gods and men.   220
Never shall the goddesses abate
their terrible wrath
until whoever sins is paid back
with evil vengeance from someone.
She also bore Righteous Anger (*Nemesis*),
a calamity for humans answerable to death,
she, destructive Night. Then she bore Deceit (*Apate*),
and Intercourse (*Philotes*), and
destructive Old Age (*Geras*), and Strife (*Eris*)
strongly competitive in spirit.   225

But hateful Strife bore
painful Hardship (*Ponos*), and
Forgetfulness (*Lethe*), and Famine (*Limos*),
and tearful Sorrows (*Algea*), and
Battles (*Hysminai*), Wars (*Machai*),
Murders (*Phonoi*) and Homicides (*Androktasiai*),
Dissension (*Nekeia*), Lies (*Pseudea*),
Arguments (*Logoi*) and Disputes (*Amphillogiai*),
Anarchy (*Dysnomia*) and Ruin (*Ate*),
two who are intimate with one another, and   230
Oath (*Horcus*), who for ground-dwelling humans
causes the most
pain, whenever one of them
willingly swears a false oath.

The Five Amazing Children of Earth and Sea

Sea (*Pontus*) sired
truthful and trusty *Nereus*,
the eldest among his children.
They call Nereus the "Old Man of the Sea"
because he reliably speaks the truth, and is gentle.
That which is right   235
is that which he never forgets.
Lawful deeds and gentle plans are the things he knows.
Then, the Sea sired great *Thaumas* (Sea Marvel)
and the headstrong Seal (*Phorcys*)
and the beautiful-cheeked Whale (*Ceto*).
All were born after the Sea slept with the Earth,
including, finally, *Eurybia*, who had in her chest
an untamed competitive spirit.

The Fifty Desirable Daughters of Doris and Nereus

Nereus sired surpassingly lovely children,
goddesses, who were born,   240
in the unplowed sea, from fair-haired *Doris*,
who was the daughter of *Ocean*,

himself the river who encircles all:
Ploto and Eucrante and Sao and *Amphitrite* and
Eudore and *Thetis* and Galene and Glauce and
Cymothoe and Speo and Thoe and lovely Halie and   245
Pasithea and Erato and rosy-armed Eunice and
graceful Melite and Eulimene and Agaue and
Doto and Proto and Pherousa and Dynamene and
Nesaea and Actaea and Protomedea,
Doris and Panopea and beauteous Galateia and   250
lovely Hippothoe and rosy-armed Hipponoe and
Cymodoce (who easily calms the waves on the dark sea
and the blasts of tempestuous winds with the help of
wave stiller Cymatolege and fair-ankled *Amphitrite*) and
Cymo and Eione and well-crowned Halimede and   255
laughter-loving Glauconome and Pontoporea and
Leagore and Euagore and Laomedea and
Polynoe and Autonoe and Lysianassa and
Euarne of lovely physique and perfect body and
Psamathe, graceful in stature, and noble Menippe and   260
Neso and Eupompe and Themisto and Pronoe and
Nemertes, who has the heart of her immortal father.
They were sired by noble Nereus,
they, fifty daughters in all, and they knew noble deeds.

The Three Flying Daughters of Electra and Thaumas

Nereus' brother, Thaumas, took
the daughter of deep-flowing Ocean,   265
Electra, as his wife.
She bore him swift *Iris*,
and then the fair-haired Harpies,
Aello (Storm Swift) and *Ocypetes* (Swift Flier),
who chase the blasts of wind.
Together with the birds
on swift wings they fly
as fast as time itself.

Five Monstrous Daughters of Ceto and Phorcys

To her brother Seal (*Phorcys*), Whale (*Ceto*) bore
fair-cheeked Gray Hags (*Graiai*).   270
Everybody calls them Gray Hags (*Graiai*)
because they were gray haired from birth.
All the immortal gods call them that,
and so do ground-dwelling humans. They are
beautifully robed *Pemphredo*
and saffron-robed *Enyo*.

She also bore the Gorgons (*Gorgoi*)
who dwell near glorious Ocean
(on the borders of Night near the pure-voiced
Hesperides, the Daughters of Evening):   275
Sthenno, *Euryale*, and *Medusa*.
Medusa suffered miseries.
She was mortal, but her sisters
were immortal and ageless.

Three Beasts Descended from Medusa and Poseidon

Spurning the two immortal sisters,
dark-haired Poseidon lay beside the singular Medusa
in a soft meadow
amid springtime blossoms.
When Perseus cut her head from
her neck, the children she had conceived,   280
the mighty *Chrysaor* and the winged
horse *Pegasus*, jumped out.
Pegasus has his name because he was born
beside the springs (*pegai*) of Ocean,
while Chrysaor was born holding
a golden sword (*chryseon aor*) in his own dear hands.
Usually beasts draw nourishment on the ground,
but Pegasus immediately flew away and
ascended to the immortals.

He dwells in the palaces of Zeus   285
and marshals the thunder and lightning for Zeus,
who is always full of stratagems.

Chrysaor sired
three-headed *Geryoneus*
after he lay with *Callirhoe*,
the daughter of famous Ocean.
With brutal violence,
Hercules killed Geryoneus
beside his cattle. They were an ambling herd
at Erythea, surrounded with water.   290
That was the day of Hercules' tenth labor.
Hercules had to herd the broad-headed cattle
to sacred Tiryns. But to get the cattle of Geryoneus
there he had to cross Ocean's path.
But first he won them by killing the monstrous
dog Orthus and the cattle driver Eurytion.
He killed the dog and herdsman in a dark stable,
on the other side of famous Ocean.

Half-Serpent Echidna, the Sixth Daughter of Phorcys

Then the Whale (*Ceto*) bore another
monstrous and inconceivable daughter.   295
She resembled nothing to be found
among mortal humans or immortal gods.
In a hollow cave, the divine and dauntless
Echnida was born.
She is one-half maiden,
a quick-glancing and fair-cheeked girl,
but also one-half monstrous
serpent, terrible and huge,
a slippery, raw-flesh eater.
She dwells beneath the sacred Earth.   300
Down below, there is a grotto
beneath the hollow rock,
far, far away from immortal gods
and mortal humans.

Down below, the gods have allotted
famous halls for her to dwell in.
Echnida, the killer, stands watch,
under the ground, in Arima,
an immortal virgin,
ageless for all days.   305

Six Monsters Descended from Echidna and Typhoeus

They say Echidna had sexual intercourse
with *Typhoeus*,
that violent and lawless monster.
He raped the quick-glancing maiden.
She became pregnant
and gave birth to bestial children.

First, she gave birth to *Orthus*,
the dog who belonged to Geryoneus, killed by Hercules.

Second, she bore an inconceivable
and unspeakable monstrosity,   310
the raw-flesh eater, *Cerberus*.
He is the bronze-voiced dog of Hades
with fifty heads,
pitiless and cruel.

Third, she gave birth to the *Hydra*,
whose fanged faces on many tentacles knew how to
deal pain. The Hydra of Lerna
was raised by white-armed Hera, as
a tool of her endless wrath, to challenge
the violent might of Hercules.   315
But Hercules, the son of Zeus,
slew her many heads with his ruthless bronze blade.
Hercules, the adopted son of Amphitryon,
had his nephew, battle-tested Iolaus, help him.
Using a strategy of Athena, winner of pillage,
he sealed Hydra's severed necks with fire.

Then Echidna bore the *Chimaera*,
who breathes unconquerable fire.
She is terrible and great.
She is swift footed and strong.   320
She has three heads.
One is that of a lion with glaring eyes,
another of a she-goat (*chimaera*),
and the last of a strong serpent snake.
The lion is in front, the serpent back behind,
and the she-goat in the middle.
She breathes out a terrible
fire of blazing wrath.
Pegasus and brave Bellerophon
took her life.   325

But Chimaera bore the destructive *Sphinx*,
doom for the Cadmeans in Thebes,
after she was raped by Orthus.
Chimaera also bore the *Lion of Nemea*,
whom Hera raised,
she, the famous spouse of Zeus.
The lion settled in the fields of Nemea,
a woe for humans.
There the lion made its home,
to perpetrate genocide.   330
The lion ruled the Nemean mountains
Tretus and Apesas, between Mycenae and Corinth.
But then one day the violent
might of Hercules struck him dead.

A Full Serpent, the Seventh Daughter of Phorcys

Then Ceto again joined with Phorcys
in sexual intercourse. She gave birth
to her youngest child, the terrible *Serpent*.
In the dark hollow of the Earth,
at the great limits, she guards

the all-golden apples of the Hesperides.   335
And now you have heard all about
the family of Ceto and Phorcys.

The Six Thousand Children of Tethys and Ocean

Tethys to *Ocean* brought forth the eddying rivers:
the *Nile* and Alpheius and deep-eddying Eridanus and
Strymon and Meander and beautifully flowing *Ister* and
Phasis and Rhesus and silver-eddying Achelous and   340
Nessus and Rhodius and Haliacmon and Heptaporus and
Granicus and Aesepus and divine Simois and
Peneus and Hermus and fair-flowing Caicus and
great Sangarius and Ladon and Parthenius and
Euenus and Ardescus and divine *Scamander.*   345

Tethys gave birth to a sacred family of daughters
who, across the Earth,
bring boys to manhood.
With the aid of Lord Apollo
and of the rivers,
they have this destiny, decreed by Zeus.

They are Peitho and Admete and Ianthe and *Electra* and
Doris and Prymno and divine-formed Urania and   350
Hippo and *Clymene* and Rhodea and *Callirhoe* and
Zeuxo and Clytie and Idyia and Pasithoe and
Plexaura and Galaxaura and charming Dione and
Melobosis and Thoe and beautiful Polydora and
Cerceis, lovely in physique, and
Pluto, with lovely large eyes, and   355
Perseis and Ianeira and Acaste and Xanthe and
charming Petraea and Menestho and *Europa* and
Metis and *Eurynome* and saffron-robed Telesto and
Chryseis and Asia and *Calypso*, who excites desire, and
Eudora and Tyche and Amphiro and Ocyrhoe and   360
Styx, who is the most preeminent of them all.

These were born of Ocean and Tethys.
These are the names of
their eldest daughters.
Yet there are many others.
Three thousand are the slender-ankled
daughters of Ocean.
Across the wide-spreading Earth
and its watery depths,   365
alike they traverse everywhere,
these glorious children of the gods.

But there is a same number of others,
of rivers flowing with sharp, loud, wet noise.
And these are not daughters, but sons of Ocean,
to whom Lady Tethys gave birth.
It is hard for a mortal man
to recount all of their names.
But if any one of them dwells in your neighborhood,
you already know the name.   370

CHAPTER 3: *Styx and Hecate*
(Aphrodite's Flood of Genealogy Ends)

The Shining Daybreak of Wisdom

Titan *Theia* gave birth to the mighty Sun (*Helius*)
and the shining Moon (*Selene*)
and the Dawn (*Eos*).
For all those on the ground, Dawn gives light.
She also gives light to the immortal gods
who rule the wide Sky.
Theia had been subdued for intercourse
by her brother Titan *Hyperion*.

Sea child *Eurybia* joined with Titan *Crius*
in intercourse, and she brought forth   375
great *Astraeus* (father of the Stars)
and *Pallas* (husband of Styx) and *Perses*,
Hecate's father, who is most conspicuous in wisdom,
since she shines among goddesses.

Dawn (*Eos*) bore to *Astraeus* (father of the Stars)
the winds strongly competitive in spirit:
the rapidly clearing *Zephyr* (West Wind) and
swift-speeding *Boreas* (North Wind) and
Notus (South Wind).
The goddess bedded with the god in intercourse.   380
Then, after the winds,
Dawn the Early Born (*Erigeneia*) gave birth to
Lucifer, the Morning Star (*Eosphorus*), and to
all the shining Stars (*Astra*) crowning Sky.

For Zeus, the Strategic Wisdom of Styx

Styx, the daughter of Ocean,
lay with *Pallas* and,

in their home, gave birth to Good Emulation (*Zelus*)
and beautiful-ankled Victory (*Nike*).

Styx also gave birth to Might (*Cratos*)
and Force (*Bia*), her very famous children.   385
These two never dwell too far from Zeus.
Neither one of them ever sits down,
or gets up to make a journey,
without the god Zeus in charge, leading them.
Zeus, who thunders loudly, always has them next to him,
knowing how to bring thunder.

Right defended by might is what Styx,
the immortal daughter of Ocean, has planned
for Zeus. She advised him on that day
when the Olympian wielder of lightning   390
had summoned the immortal gods
to assemble on lofty Olympus. On her advice,
Zeus said that anyone among the gods
who would fight with him against the Titans
shall not be deprived of any honors.
Anyone among them who would fight
shall retain whatever privilege
they previously held among the immortal gods.

Zeus also said anyone who, under Cronus,
was dishonored and without privilege   395
shall obtain privilege and honors.
Such advancement would be what is right.

Styx, the immortal daughter of Ocean,
was the first to defect to the side of Olympus,
together with her children, in accordance with
the stratagem of her dear father, Ocean.
In return, Zeus granted her a privilege.
He gave her extraordinary gifts.
He established that she would be
the great oath of the gods.   400
And her children would dwell with him
for all the days to come.

Similarly too does he maintain right,
forever, for all. Exactly what he promised is what
he did. It is Zeus who, by deploying great might
judiciously, is Lord, forever, over all.

For Mortals, the Gentle Gifts of Hecate

Phoebe went to
Coeus' much-loved bed.
Then the goddess, conceiving a daughter
in intercourse with the god,   405
gave birth to her, *Leto*, the dark-robed one.
Leto is always gentle
and mild, both to humans
and to immortal gods.
She has been gentle right from the beginning.
Of all those on Olympus, she is most kind.

Then, Phoebe gave birth to *Asteria*,
whose name is revered. It is Asteria whom *Perses*
led into his great house,
to be called his dear spouse.   410
Asteria became pregnant and gave birth
to *Hecate*. To Hecate, above all others,
has Zeus, the son of Cronus, granted a privilege.
He has given her glorious gifts.
To her is assigned a portion of the Earth,
and of the Sea (which cannot be harvested),
and of the starry Sky,
as her honor.
Especially honored is she,
by the immortal gods.   415

Even now, when any human
who dwells on the ground
offers beautiful sacrifices
according to custom
to become reconciled with the gods
he invokes Hecate.

Many privileges will be obtained by him
easily, he whose prayers
the goddess is glad and eager
to receive. She will send him beatitude.
It is within her power.   420

Among those who came forth from Earth and Sky,
however many there are who received privilege,
she is one of them,
one who has received her share.
Zeus, the son of Cronus,
never forced from her, or robbed her of,
what she had obtained from the Titans,
who ruled before Zeus.
She kept whatever had been distributed
in the way it was first done.   425

As for the new honors Zeus assigned to her
among Earth and Sea and Sky,
although she is an only child, a mere girl,
even so, Hecate has not been honored with less.
Rather, she has been given so very much more.
Such is the way Zeus honors this girl.

Whomever she wishes,
she mightily assists with great benefits.
Bringing justice is she,
enthroned with venerable kings.   430
She is conspicuous among people in the marketplace.
A fair deal for the one she chooses!
Whenever men put on their armor,
to face war's bloody slaughter,
at that moment, the goddess is present,
for those whom she wishes.
She eagerly joins such men as victory's companion.
To them, she extends glory.
Bravely does she stand in battle,
close by her chosen knights.   435

Bravery is hers too for men who,
in peacetime, struggle for prizes.
In all their contests, she assists them
with great benefits.
He who wins, although he had used
power and might, now receives the prize,
the beautiful prize, gently and gracefully.
Such a winner also brings glory to his parents.

To those men who work the silvery sea,
rough and stormy,   440
if they pray to Hecate, and to Poseidon,
the loud-sounding Earth Shaker,
then easily does the goddess send
abundance, the proud catch.
Easily too could she take away, in a competitive spirit,
anything good approaching.

With good luck (bringing it on like *Hermes*),
she increases the livestock in the pens.
Herds of cattle,
wide flocks of goats, and   445
droves of wooly sheep:
depending on how competitive her spirit is,
she magnifies the small.
But she could turn the great into so much less.

And so, even though Hecate is
her mother's only child, a mere girl,
among all the immortals, she is granted
a privilege, along with all her other honors:
Zeus, the son of Cronus,
has made her
Governess of All Children.

Every child
born into the world
after Hecate was born,

every child
whose eyes
see
the portion of light   450
granted in Dawn's gentle radiance,
witnesses it:
an ancient honor,
in the Sky,
apportioned
to the Governess,
by the Stygian wisdom of
the Zeusfather,
he who was born to govern.

Every child who sees the new day's light
owes thanks to them both.

CHAPTER 4: *Stealing Thunder*
(The Succession Myth, Part 2)

The Birth of Zeus

Rhea, raped by Cronus,
gave birth to her famous children:
Hestia (Hearth Goddess);
and *Demeter* (Earth Mother);
and *Hera* of golden sandals;
and *Hades* the powerful,
who dwells in palaces beneath the hard ground 455
with a likewise hard heart;
and *Poseidon*, the Earth Shaker, who rumbles loudly;
and *Zeus*, full of stratagems.
The Zeusfather of gods and husbands is he,
by whose thunder
the broad ground trembles.
But great Cronus quaffed them
to quell them. As each one emerged
out from her sacred womb
and reached the mother's knees, 460
he resolved in his mind
that not one of these noble children, descendants of the Sky,
would arrogate his honor.
Nobody else among the immortals would be King.
He had learned the openly obvious from the Earth
and the Sky, sparkled with stars.
For a husband like him, it was unavoidable.
A child would overthrow him. He knew,
no matter how mighty Cronus was,
deliberate action by a great god would win out. 465
Not blind to the threat, therefore,
he kept watch, with keen anticipation.
As they were born, he quaffed them
to quell them. Rhea's pain, however, was unerasable.

And so, when she was about to give birth
to the Zeusfather of gods and husbands,
her last and youngest child,
she implored her own dear parents, the Earth
and the Sky, sparkled with stars,   470
to devise, together with her, a stratagem
so that she could give birth
in hiding
to her dear son.
Then, one day, his father would face the vengeful spirit
of his children, they whom Cronus
(in a famously evil stratagem) quaffed to quell.
Listening to their daughter,
they were persuaded.
They made clear to her
what must happen unavoidably   475
for Cronus, the King
who was strongly competitive in spirit.
They sent Rhea to Lyctus,
a fertile district of Crete,
when she was about to give birth
to the youngest of her children,
great Zeus. Gigantic Earth herself
was there to hold him at birth. There
in wide Crete did the Earth nourish
and raise him for Rhea.   480
Rhea had to travel there in haste,
conveying Zeus under cover of black night.
First, she arrived pregnant in Lyctus.
Then, after she held him in her hands,
she hid him deep in a cave,
deep within the hollows of sacred Earth,
deep beneath the Aegean mountain, dense with woodland.

The Counterfeit Stone

Back at home, she wrapped a large stone
in swaddling clothes, and handed him over   485
to the Great Lord, the Son of the Sky

(the Sky formerly known as King of the Gods).
Cronus seized it then with his hands.
He incited Rhea to sow that stone inside,
he, abominable Cronus. She delighted:
he didn't know the son outside.
Replaced by a stone, her son still lived,
unconquered. Consequently, Cronus cared not
that someone might yet overthrow him and,
with a violent hand,   490
remove his honor from him.
His honor, amid the immortals, was to be their Lord.

Swiftly did strength
in the noble limbs
of the hidden Lord grow.
When one year had passed,
on Earth's shrewd advice,
Cronus was tricked to ingest an emetic.
Cronus (despite his famously evil stratagem)
then vomited up his offspring.   495
As he retched, he knew he would be conquered
by the skill and might of a son.

First, Cronus vomited the stone out.
It was the last thing he had quaffed.
Zeus fixed it later in the wide-open ground,
for the Pythian oracle
at sacred Delphi,
under the mountain glens of Parnassus.
Ever since, the rock remains sign of his rule,
a wondrous attraction for mortals to see.   500

Next, Zeus freed his father's brothers,
the Cyclopes, from their deadly chains.
They too were unwanted sons of Sky.
But how thoughtlessly did father Sky bind them!
Returning the kindnesses of Zeus,
they showed gratitude.
The Cyclopes gave Zeus the thunder,
the smoldering bolt, the lightning.

Previously, these weapons had been locked away
in the vast Earth, inside Tartarus.   505
Now, thanks to these trusty weapons,
Zeus is Lord, over mortals and immortals alike.

CHAPTER 5: *Sacrifice; or, The Counterparts*

The Four Stiff-Necked Children of Iapetus

Iapetus married Ocean's daughter,
the one with the delicate ankles,
Clymene. Into the same bed they climbed.
She gave birth to her child *Atlas* (Sky Pillar),
a strong-willer. She bore more
like him: famous, all-too-famous,
Menoetius (Might for Nought); 510
Prometheus, dappled and devious (Fore-Thought);
and mistake-minded *Epimetheus* (After-Thought),
who, in the beginning, took her,
Pandora,
an evil to men. Now they work for food.

The Punishments of Rivalry

Epimetheus felt special, as the first one
to take home a woman. But recall: Zeus made the maiden.
And it was Zeus, a long-range thinker,
who threw violent *Menoetius* down
into the Darkness.
He tumbled down like lightning, 515
due punishment for recklessness.
Excessive competitiveness ever ends thus.
Show-off *Atlas* proudly holds up the Sky.
But he shoulders compulsion's heavy burden.
At Earth's borders, he can hear
the pure voices of the Daughters of Evening (*Hesperides*).
And so he stands with head and arms that never grow tired,
thinking he impresses them.
This is the fate, a trick,
which Zeus did allot for him. 520

But *Prometheus*, smarter than all that,
was the sole case needing inescapable chains.
Bonds of pure pain,
right through the middle, fastened to a pillar.
Under the wide wings' shadow,
upon him it descends, and eats his liver.
The eagle eats forever.
Because what grows back during the night
matches what the bird eats all day long,
under the wide wings' shadow.   525

Finally, he killed it: he, the brave one,
son of Alcmene (she another with delicate ankles),
Hercules, he who culls
all evil plagues.
By him, Iapetus' son Prometheus
was freed from suffering,
and not against the will of Olympian Zeus,
whose grand strategy had mortals in mind,
that the fame of half-mortal Hercules
and of his hometown, Thebes,   530
would extend far across the earth,
as far as it nourishes those who work for food.
Because this was his mind, Zeus honored his son.
And who hasn't heard of Hercules?

Unbinding anger. That was Zeus' way of ending
the anger Prometheus himself unbound
when Prometheus tried to outwit
the almighty son of Cronus.

Counterparts; or, The Story of Sacrifice

In the beginning, the division between gods
and mortals was decided   535
at Mecone, where Prometheus,
in a competitive mood (as usual), chopped
up a big ox and, seeking to outwit
the mind of Zeus, arranged the parts this way:

to mortals, Prometheus assigned the meat
along with the inner skins juicy with fat.
But he hid them beneath
the unappetizing stomach of the ox.
To Zeus, Prometheus assigned
the inedible white ox bones. But in a skillful ruse   540
he hid them beneath glistening fat,
making them look good.
Yet, at that very moment,
the Zeusfather of husbands and gods spoke out:

"Son of Iapetus, among all who rule,
you stand out in notoriety,
but yet, noble sir, have you really
divided the portions here fairly?"

So said Zeus, whose stratagems never end,
with his irony testing Prometheus.   545
But sharp-witted Prometheus spoke out,
and with a hint of a smile,
playing out his skillful ruse,
turned the test back on Zeus:

"Zeus, most lauded Zeus,
greatest among all the gods who live forever,
if you insist on seeing this in a competitive frame of mind,
then please, take your pick."

So said Prometheus, feigning magnanimity.
Zeus, whose stratagems never end,   550
recognized the ruse. He was not blind
to Prometheus' intentions. Zeus even foresaw
the evils that from competition would extend
unto dying humans. So he knew what to do.
With both hands, he held up the pile of white fat,
making his choice with a flourish.
So that division would always enkindle anger
on both sides, he let competitive anger
rush over him, when he saw,
under the skillful ruse, the white ox bones.   555

And this is why now, upon the ground,
every human tribe burns, to the deathless ones,
white bones on altars, pouring forth smoke
in sacrifices, clouds vying with one another.
With his wrath now enkindled,
Zeus the cloud gatherer spoke out:

"Son of Iapetus, you know
stratagems like no one else,
but yet, noble sir, the skillful ruse
has not yet been played out to its finish."   560
So spoke Zeus, whose stratagems never end,
as he would let the anger, taken up, unwind.

The Fire of Retaliation

From that moment on, Zeus, aflame,
kept memory of the ruse in mind.
He would not grant the power
of ever-dancing fire to strike, in lightning,
the ash trees. That would benefit humans,
the ones who die, who dwell on the ground.
And so Prometheus, the noble
son of Iapetus, lied to him   565
and stole ever-dancing fire,
the flash seen from afar.
He hid it in the hollow of a giant fennel plant,
the narthex. A newly competitive sting
then struck Zeus, whose thunder crashes from heaven.
His friendly heart let anger in
when he saw among humans
the flash seen from afar: fire.

Woman; or, The Crown of Creatures

Right away, as a counterpart to the good of fire,
for humans he made an evil.   570
From the Earth (*Gaia*), *Hephaestus*,

the famous lame god, put together
(according to the blueprints of Zeus, the son of Cronus)
what looked like a modest virgin.
The steely-eyed goddess, Athena,
herself dressed and adorned the girl
with clothes of silver. From the top of her head,
a veil cascaded,
decorated by the hands of Athena,
framing the marvel of the maiden's face. 575
Placed on her head were garlands,
the blossoms of fresh growth.
Everything desirable, just as it is found
in the virgin goddess, Pallas Athena.
Athena also placed around the girl's head
a crown of gold.
The famous lame god, Hephaestus,
himself had made it.
He handcrafted it,
as a special favor to his father, Zeus. 580
On it, many intricate details were fashioned.
They were marvels to see.
Choosing from among all the many creatures
nourished by land and sea,
he included the greater part.
Grace animated each one, and they shone out
marvelously. It was as if these animals were alive
and spoke with voices.

Marriage; or, The Ultimate Counterpart

After Hephaestus had fashioned her,
as a beautiful evil, the counterpart to noble fire, 585
out he led her, out to where all the others
had gathered, gods and humans.
Adorned like steely-eyed Athena, daughter of the mighty
father Zeus, she delighted them.
So marvelous was she, she transfixed the gods, immortal,
and humans, the ones who die.
They saw in her the ultimate ruse,

from which humans can devise no escape.
From her comes the race of women,
from her all human females.   590
Destructive is that race,
the tribe of wives.

They dwell among mortal husbands
as their great pain.
They do not hang about in destructive Poverty.
They are sharers only of Plenty.
Similarly, yet conversely, do the female bees
bring, into the shelter of the hive,
food for the male drones who, in evil deeds,
are their counterparts.   595
All day long,
until the sun goes down,
the bees busy themselves
and fill the honeycombs with honey white.
Meanwhile, the drones, staying home
within the shelter of the nest,
place into their stomachs
what was earned by the toil of others.
In the same way,
wives are an evil for mortal men.   600

Zeus, whose thunder crashes from heaven,
established them as counterparts, since their
deeds are troublesome. To those thinking
it good to avoid them, Zeus added another evil.
He who flees marriage
and the vexing deeds of wives,
he who chooses not to marry,
arrives at devastating old age
without anyone to tend to him.
He takes care of himself   605
while he's alive.
But when he dies, who divides up his estate?
Distant relatives, that's who.

Yet for he who comes to accept that his fate is to marry,
to have a cherished spouse,
hearts joined together in gratitude …

Even so, to that noble goodness
somehow there will be, matched eternally, some evil
that abides. Yet it could have been worse.
If he had married an annoying wife,   610
he would live with
an incessant distress in his chest,
angrily competitive and sick in heart.
And only that sort of evil is truly deadly.

Captivating Mind; or, The Ultimate Stratagem

All of this proves that nobody, not even Prometheus,
can steal from the mind of Zeus
and bypass his will. For not even
the son of Iapetus, Prometheus, that special case,
was able to escape the punishment of the heaviest anger.
Instead, beneath necessity,   615
no matter how many cures raw mind would contrive,
the ancient ball and chain restrains.

CHAPTER 6: *Battle of the Titans*
(The Succession Myth, Part 3)

The Liberation of the Hundred-Handers;
or, A New Battle Plan

What happened first was that father Cronus
felt the sting of competition from *Obriareus*
and *Cottus* and *Gyges*, the Hundred-Handers.
So he bound them in strong chains.
He thought he had to do this
because of their overwhelming prowess.
How they looked. How big they were.
So he installed them beneath the broad ground.   620
Painfully did they dwell there, beneath the ground,
at the lowest point, inside Earth's great boundary,
grieving very much, and
holding great sorrow in their heart.
But the son of Cronus, Zeus, plotted
with the other deathless gods, the Olympians
to whom rich-haired Rhea gave birth
from her intercourse with Cronus.   625
Acting on the shrewdness of the Earth,
Zeus freed them, and they saw the light again.
Earth had explained in detail to Zeus and the Olympians
everything they needed to know:
only with the Hundred-Handers could they carry off
the victory, and win wide fame.

Seeing the Light; or, The Force Multiplier Effect

They had been fighting for much too long.
A painfully competitive labor it was, the war
between the gods known as the Titans,
and those born of Cronus, the Olympians.   630
Between these two sides,

the mighty battle continued to rage.
Wondrous were the Titans,
with their headquarters high up on Mount Othrys.
But camped on Mount Olympus were the gods,
those who now give blessings to us,
those to whom rich-haired Rhea gave birth
after she lay with Cronus.
Painfully competitive was the wrath
they had against one another.   635
Without pause,
they had fought ten full years.
With no backing down from dangerous strife,
yet with no decisive battle
for either side, the only achievement of the war
had been prolonged war.
But then Zeus supplied the Hundred-Handers
with just what they needed.
Nectar to drink. Ambrosia to eat.
The diet of the gods themselves.   640
It fed the brave competitive spirit
within all their chests.
Thus did they taste the charms
of nectar and ambrosia.

Then the Zeusfather of husbands and gods
 spoke to them, in their midst, as ally to ally:
"Listen to me now, splendid children
 of Earth and Sky (*Gaia* and *Uranus*).
The competitive spirit in my chest
 urges me to say these things: 645
already for far too long now,
aligned against one another,
every day, we have been battling
to the end, for supreme victory,
the twelve Titan gods
versus the six children of Cronus.
I want you, with your great brute force,
with your unstoppable hands,
to show the Titans, head-on,
what truly deadly battle looks like.   650

Look at how well we get along.
Remember how much you used to suffer.
Now in the light, you see things clearly.
You are free from the painful chains.
And that is our battle plan:
to dispel confusion, to remove the darkness."

So said Zeus.
And noble Cottus replied in turn:
"Divine Zeus, you make things clear,
  things of which we have not been unaware.   655
And we ourselves admit your superiority,
  both in tactical mind and strategic purpose.
You have defended us, immortals,
  from a cold doom.
Indeed, your plan has dispelled the confusion.
You removed us from the darkness.
Back again,
  freed from hard chains,
we come to you, Lord, son of Cronus.
This is our experience of hopes surpassed.   660
Therefore, with earnest intent
and after careful deliberation,
in this deadly battle, we declare ourselves
  the allies of your power.
We will fight against the Titans,
  in combat, strafing them."

So said Cottus. And the gods,
they who give blessings to us, gave hearty acclamation
  when they heard this speech.
Their competitive spirit desired victory in war,   665
  even more so than it had before.
And so they initiated a dreadful battle
  on that same day. All of them,
female and male, joined the fight:
  the twelve Titan gods
versus the six children of Cronus
now joined by those Zeus had brought,
from the underground Darkness, into the light.

Terrible and mighty were they.
They held overwhelming force.   670
One hundred hands
whirled out from the shoulders
on each one of them.
And each one of them had fifty heads
grown up above their shoulders.
Strong were their arms.

The Battle of the Titans

Ready for grim war,
they lined up against the Titans.
In their strong hands,
they held massive rocks.   675
On the other side,
the Titans continued to fortify their battle line
in eager anticipation.
They displayed might and manpower simultaneously
on both sides. Then a terrible echo sounded out
across the limitless waters:
the Earth roared loudly,
and the wide Sky groaned
as it shook, because lofty Olympus itself
was shaking right at its foot,   680
as the immortals began to clash.
The heavy quake reached even
opaque Tartarus.
So too the high-pitched howling
of the indescribable fray,
of the screaming of stones thrown.
They took aim for pain;
and, letting fly, both sides hit the mark.
Then cries ricocheted
across the starry Sky on both sides   685
as they charged.
They hurtled together with a loud yell.

And this was the point
where Zeus held nothing back.
While keeping his mind in steady control,
he unveiled unchecked
violence. Down from the Sky,
down from Olympus,
he strode forth on a carpet of lightning.
In a burst of bolts,   690
the thunder and lightning
enfiladed the Titans
under the sweep of his steady hands.
The holy flood
flashed.
Usually the Earth gives life, but now it screamed,
set aflame. Her vast forests encircled her
with crackling fires.
The heat of the ground
boiled Ocean's streams   695
and boiled the sea. A plow won't harm it,
but boiling can. Also vulnerable
to this swirling heat? The Titans.
Was not the Earth their mother? The fire climbed
up over them too, into the air. With eyes blind,
it doesn't matter how strong you are.
And the dazzling flashes
of unbolted lightning blinded them.

So hot was the heat that it reached down
to Chaos, the womb of the Earth.   700
If you could have seen all this
with your own eyes, or heard it with your ears,
it would have seemed just as if the Earth
and the wide Sky above
had themselves collided.
How loud the noise would be
if the Earth got slammed, fallen upon
by the Sky from above. That's
how loud the noise was when Zeus crashed down
and clashed with the Titans.   705

Then came the winds. They made more things shake.
They made more storms of dust.
This weather shift amplified the thunder,
augmented the lightning, the flashing bolt –
all the weapons of great Zeus.
The wind blowing this way, a path in the middle opened
for a direct assault. With a shout,
the signal was given.

The deadly charge was made.
That moment's picture is eternal: the brave gambit,   710
overturning the tipping point.
Up until that day, the gods had assaulted one another
indecisively, the war prolonged
by their assaults equally strong.

But on that day, the shift came,
when they stepped to the front of the charge, they,
Cottus and *Briareus* and *Gyges*,
new allies with outsized appetite for revenge.
Three hundred rocks,
under the sweep of their steady hands,   715
poured forth in rapid succession.
Like the sudden descent of a shadow, they enfiladed
the Titans. In this Hundred-Handed shadow,
the Titans beneath the broad ground
were sent. And that is how the Titans
came to be bound below with painful bonds.
The Titans had a competitive, all-too competitive, spirit.
It took many hands to beat them.

How far below the Earth were they bound?
How far the Sky is from the Earth,   720
that's how far the Earth is
from opaque Tartarus.
Nine nights and days,
a bronze anvil,
falling down from the Sky,
would reach the Earth on the tenth.
Nine nights and days,
a bronze anvil,
falling down into the Earth,
would reach Tartarus on the tenth.   725
A bronze prison wall marks off Tartarus.
Night beneath
swirls around its neck in a triple choke hold.
But touching on top
are the roots of the Earth,
which grow upward into the sea, where no plow can go.

Down below, in the opaque netherworld,
the Titan gods
have been hidden away,
by decision of Zeus the cloud gatherer,   730
in a rotting corner,
in the extremities of terrible Earth.
There is no way to exit.
Poseidon shut them in with doors
made of bronze,
and a wall installed on both sides.

Down there, Gyges and Cottus and Obriareus,
greatly competitive in spirit, again
dwell, not as prisoners,
but as trusted prison guards, under the aegis of Zeus.   735

48

Down even farther,
dark Earth and opaque Tartarus
and Sea, where no plow can go,
and Sky, sparkled with stars,
each terminate
at four points of origin,
in slimy pits abhorred
especially by the gods,
in a great chasm.
Not even if you kept going to the end of the tenth year   740
could you reach the chasm's floor.
Even if, beginning the tenth year,
you managed to pass by Tartarus' gates,
hurricanes would then blow you in circles
endlessly, a punishment so terrible
that even the immortal gods dare not step forth
into that monstrous chasm.
Fixed within is the terrible home of dark Night,
but no one may look upon it,
past the veil of those dark hurricane clouds.   745

One step back from all these places
is where Atlas, Iapetus' son, holds the wide Sky
on his head with his tireless hands.
He stands firm
and does not flinch when Night and Day draw near
to that spot and, as they pass,
greet one another,
changing places across Tartarus' great threshold
of bronze. Coming inside, the one will go down,
but the other, heading outside,   750
quickly departs.
Both of them will not be cooped up inside that house.
Instead, one of the two, leaving the house behind,
travels abroad,
wending across the Earth.
The other, waiting inside the house,
counts down the hours to her journey,
right until the moment arrives.

For those who dwell on the ground,
the one carries long-ranging light.   755
But the other brings in her hands Sleep,
Death's brother.
That other is Night,
and she is deadly under dark-clouded veil.

Down below,
dark Night's children also have houses, for
Sleep and Death are also terrible gods.
Never upon them
does the shining Sun
make beaming faces,   760
not when he goes up the Sky,
not when he comes down the Sky.

Day goes back into Earth
and wide-ridged waters,
pivoting leisurely.
She treats humans gently.
But Night's intent is iron,
and her heart is like bronze-encircled Tartarus,
a pitiless chest.
Neither one ever wants to let you go, and   765
no human can escape.
Hated are they, even by the immortal gods.

Down below, in front of the hollow homes
of the underground god,
of powerful Hades and
of his dread wife, Persephone,
there stands a terrible dog,
Cerberus, guarding the gates.
He ruthlessly repeats the same evil ruse.
To those entering,   770
he's harmless:
he wags his tail, and flops his ears.
But try and go back again, and he won't allow it.
Lying in ambush,
he chews to pieces

anyone he catches heading for the gates
of powerful Hades and
of his dread wife, Persephone.

Down below, there dwells a goddess
the immortals think abominable,   775
terrible Styx,
the daughter of Ocean (he to whom all rivers return),
his eldest daughter.
Set apart from the gods, she dwells in famous halls
with tall rocks standing overhead.
All around her,
silver pillars have been erected,
pointing to the Sky.

On rare occasions, fast-footed *Iris*,
the daughter of Thaumas,   780
goes as a messenger back and forth to Sky,
traveling over the wide-ridged waters.
Whenever among the immortals
conflicts and quarrels arise,
because a god who lives in the palaces of Olympus
is suspected of telling lies,
Zeus sends Iris to bring
the great oath test for the gods.
She brings it from afar, in a golden jar.
This water goes by many names.   785
It is cold, like cold truth.
Its waterfall trickles down from a steep rock,
down from a high top.
From far beneath the ground's broad path,
it arrives there, under the cover of black Night.
It comes from a sacred river
branching off from Ocean,
he who allots it one-tenth of his water.
The other nine parts keep on flowing around Earth,
her wide-ridged waters fed   790
by the silver eddies
swirling into her salt water.
But this tenth part trickles down from the steep rock:
Styx, she sticks it to the gods.

Whoever pours this water in libation,
and then perjures himself,
that immortal,
although blessed to live on the snowy peaks of Olympus,
will nonetheless stop breathing
until one year has passed.   795
He will be unable, therefore,
to enjoy ambrosia and nectar
as his food. Instead he will lay without breath,
unable to speak.
An evil coma will conceal him,
keeping him tucked in bed.
But when, after one year,
this great sickness passes,
another ordeal is added to this one,
an even harsher ordeal.   800
For the next nine years,
he is deprived of the company of the gods who live forever.
He is not allowed to join them
in their deliberations or at their feasts.
Nine whole years must pass.
In the tenth, he may join them again
in the assembly hall of the immortals,
they who have palaces on Mount Olympus.
For this oath test, Styx's water
was established by the gods as imperishable   805
back in the earliest times.
That is why its water falls in the rugged place, Tartarus.

Down even farther,
dark Earth and opaque Tartarus
and Sea, where no plow can go,
and Sky, sparkled with stars,
each terminate
at four points of origin,
in slimy pits abhorred
especially by the gods.   810

Always remember,
the marble wall and bronze doors, down below,
will never fall,
because Poseidon had them installed alive, with long roots
self-growing magically.
Imprisoned inside, cut off from all the other gods,
the Titans are compelled to dwell.
Their only neighbor is Chaos, the Void.

But the allies of Zeus (he who brings loud thunder)
were celebrated with honors.   815
They dwell now in palaces
right at Ocean's foundations,
they, Cottus and Gyges.
As for Briareus, because he was so brave,
Poseidon, the loud-pounding Earth Shaker,
made him son-in-law.
He awarded him the hand in marriage of his daughter
Cymopolea (the Wave Walker).

The Typhoeus War

After Zeus banished the Titans,
now forbidden to show their faces to the Sky,   820
gigantic Earth gave birth
to her youngest child, Typhoeus.
(Some say she had, due to Aphrodite's golden charms,
had intercourse with Tartarus.)
Mighty are his hands.
Mighty are his exploits.
Sturdy are his feet.
Strong is the god. On his shoulders:
one hundred serpent heads.
He is a terrible dragon.   825
One hundred black tongues lash out.
Out from his eyes,
from beneath the brows on his awful heads,
fire darts.
Whenever he looks around,
all of his whirling heads send jets of fire.
From each terrible head,
animal sounds come forth.
Indescribable is their variety of screams.
Sometimes   830
when they howl, the gods can translate the language.
Sometimes the only voice heard is
a bull crying
with unrestrained force and unstoppable pride, or
sometimes a pitiless lion crying out
with competitive spirit, or
sometimes a hundred puppies yelping,
incredible to hear, or
sometimes the serpents simply hiss,
which the mountaintops echo back.   835

That day of Typhoeus' birth
could have been an inescapable turning point.
Typhoeus would have become Lord
over mortals and immortals both,
but the Zeusfather of husbands and gods
foresaw that Typhoeus would try to depose him.

And so he thundered hard and heavy.
Across all the Earth,
the terrifying sound echoed.
It echoed into the wide Sky above,   840
then across Ocean's sea and streams,
and down into Tartarus, below the Earth.
Beneath the god's immortal feet,
great Olympus shook
as Lord Zeus sprang into action.
The Earth began to groan.
Then a flash of heat, from Zeus and Typhoeus,
penetrated the deep-blue Sea.
His thunder and lightning
clashed with that monster's fire blasts.   845
Spinning his heads, typhoon winds from Typhoeus
scattered Zeus' flashing bolts.

The scattered bolts made the whole ground
boil up. Sky and waters too.
Tidal waves smashed the shores,
encircling all, engulfing all,
side effects of the immortals' rage.
Then an unstoppable earthquake began.
Even Hades, lord of the dead below,
was shaken.   850
Even the Titans, below in Tartarus,
who once fearlessly flanked Cronus in battle line,
were knocked into disarray
by the never-ending roar of this horrible strife.

At last, Zeus raised high his wrath.
His weapons, he fully deployed:
thunder, lightning,

and the smoking bolt.
Leaping from Olympus into the air,
he struck in all directions,   855
raining down burning fire,
torching each prodigious head of the terrible monster.
Then he broke his body,
with bone-crushing blows.
Typhoeus, now crippled,
Zeus now toppled. And gigantic Earth groaned.

Smoldering with Zeus' lightning fires,
toppled Typhoeus spread flame.
The dark mountain crags lit up,
glens ablaze   860
where Typhoeus fell.
The greater part of gigantic Earth caught fire.

Under incredible heat,
she melted, as tin melts
under the craftsman's skill,
in the crucible's blast,
when it is heated.
She melted as the strongest iron melts
when, forged under blazing fire,
inside the mountain,   865
under glowing ground,
the palms of Hephaestus bend it at will.
So too did Earth melt, so too did she bend,
beneath the glow of Zeus' blazing fires.
Grieving at the cost of such a competitive spirit,
Zeus cast Typhoeus into wide Tartarus.

Evil Winds; or, The Children of Typhoeus

Typhoeus is father of all wet winds,
evil in their mighty blasts.
Notus and Boreas, however,
and the rapidly clearing Zephyr, are good winds.   870
They are born from good gods, Astraeus and Eos.

They are a great help to mortals.
But Typhoeus' evil winds
blow random squalls over the waters.
They assault
the misty sea,
a great plague for mortals,
as their evil storms rage.
They blow unpredictably,
smashing ships and   875
scattering sailors.
Bravery is a useless defense against them
for the unlucky men
who meet them upon the sea.
They even invade
the boundless expanses of flowering Earth,
destroying the beloved works of humans,
who (unlike them) were born on the ground.
Typhoeus' children, with dust and tumult,
remind us now of anarchy's ancient threat.   880

CHAPTER 9: *The Insider*

The Election of Zeus

The blessed gods had thus put an end to the war.
The hard work of
adjudicating the Titans' arrogated honors
had been decided by force.
Now they demanded, by acclamation,
that their King and Lord
(even shrewd Earth agreed) ought to be Olympian Zeus,
the long-range thinker
who, among all the immortals,
has proven that he can distribute honors justly.   885

Zeus Swallows Metis
(Wisdom Inside – Better Than Castration Outside)

When he became King of gods,
Zeus took *Metis* (Practical Wisdom)
as his first wife.
When it comes to dealing with mortal humans,
she knows the most.
But when Metis was about to give birth
to the steely-eyed goddess, *Athena*,
then, on the spot,
Zeus led the fluid mind of Metis his way,
with an inviting ruse.
In words that flattered, he invited Metis,
Ocean's daughter,
to flow as one inside: 890
a shrewdly consensual move,
inspired by the love gone awry
with Earth and starry Sky.

Those two made clear how to avoid
challenges from offspring,
so that the honor of King
would be held by none of the gods
(who, once born, live forever),
none, other than Zeus.
Rivalry was unavoidable.
From Metis,
only very intelligent children could ever be born.
Luckily, her first was a daughter:
steely-eyed Athena, born by the river Triton.   895
The equal of her father Zeus,
she possesses both careful deliberation and firm resolve.

But these qualities, in a son,
would make him want to be
the new King of gods and men.
So, before Metis gave birth again,
Zeus pre-emptively banished all lawlessness of heart.
Before she to son,
he to her
gave pride of place.
He invited Metis
to flow as one inside.
Now the goddess makes clear to him
good and evil:
she, the consummate insider.   900

Hesiod's *Works*

INTRODUCTION: *A Prayer to Zeus*

O Muses, it is in song
that you bring glory.
From your perch near Pieria, come here now.
In hymns, you tell us of your father, Zeus.
Next to him, mortal husbands
are not worth speaking about, except when they are.

The will of great Zeus decides
who will be famous, and who not.
Easy does he raise up the mighty.
But easy does he wear down the proud.   5

Yes, easy does he knock the famous down.
Yet easy does he make famous the unknown.
So easy does he make the crooked straight.
So easy does he make the arrogant afraid.
He is Zeus, who sends this thunder from on high.
In the loftiest palaces, he rightly dwells.

O Zeus, you see and hear all. Hear my prayer.
Only your justice makes our laws straight.
Let me use Musical storytelling
to speak these real truths that Perses needs to hear.   10

CHAPTER 1: *The Good Strife*

There is more than one kind of Strife (*Eris*).
Look all over the Earth (*Gaia*), and
see there are two. Consider:
one kind of Strife is praiseworthy;
the other kind is blameworthy.
Each kind has a completely different competitive spirit.

One kind multiplies evils,
in wars and battles.
She is the cruel Strife.
No mortal loves her. Only under compulsion   15
(the design of the immortals) do mortals honor
the heavy burden she imposes.

But dark Night (*Nyx*) gave birth
to the other kind of Strife first.
Zeus, the son of Cronus, enthroned on high,
dwelling in the sky, placed this Strife
in the roots of the Earth.
She is much more beneficial for men.
However helpless anyone may be,
equally does she instigate each one to work.   20

Consider the man who is without work.
What if he looks at somebody else?
He will see the rich man. He will see a field earnestly plowed.
Then it is planted.

Look at the well-ordered household. Why did that happen?
Neighbor imitated neighbor.
As if in a race, they acquired possessions.
Yes, this kind of Strife is good for mortals.

How is the best anger fired up?
By potter against potter. By artist against artist.   25
Who can hold the productive grudge?

Poor man against poor man. Bard against bard.
O Perses, my brother, make these, then,
the concerns for your competitive spirit.

Don't let Strife keep your competitive spirit
from work. Don't rejoice in evil-doing
by being a spectator to quarrels,
a partisan hearer in the public assembly.
There is little time left
for quarrels and assemblies   30
if you worry instead about being at home,
storing up enough to live on for a year.
Timely and in season, from the goddess, Demeter,
the Earth brings us her gift, grain.

But if you haven't earned a sufficient livelihood,
then you have no business advancing
quarrels and disputes for someone else's possessions.
Yet such is your irrevocable attack.
You've done what you've done, haven't you?
Well, let us settle the quarrel, right now,   35
with frank judgments. And frank judgments,
done in the style of Zeus, are the best:

We already divided our inheritance.
But half wasn't enough for you. Much more than that
did you steal from me. Because you flattered kings,
you took from me large amounts.
You fed them bribes, and they chose to adjudicate
with judgment in your favor.
Idiots! One plus one is two!
But they allowed you to steal more than my half from me.   40
Next bribe required: laxatives, toilet paper.
Relief for the judge stuffed with all your crap!

CHAPTER 2: *Pandora*

And the gods? They have sufficient livelihood.
But they've hidden it all from humans.
Otherwise we'd have it easy.
We would only need to work for one day.
One day, and we'd have enough for the whole year.
We'd take all the other days off.
One, then farm tools quickly useless,
except as trophies mounted above the fireplace.   45
Oxen and mules: they worked a hard day.
But now they'd have to find a new occupation.

It was Zeus who hid sufficient livelihood from us.
He used anger, according to his plan.
The plan was a response to Prometheus,
who tried to deceive him with a wily stratagem.
Because of Prometheus, Zeus was able to unfold
his plan for humans: troublesome toils.

Yes, Zeus hid fire.
In retaliation, Prometheus, the noble son of Iapetus,   50
stole it for humans from Zeus.
A fateful move, because Zeus is full of stratagems.
Prometheus hid it from Zeus, in the hollow of the narthex.
But Zeus loves to thunder.
With his wrath now enkindled,
Zeus the cloud gatherer spoke out:

"Son of Iapetus,
you know stratagems like no one else.
You delight in stealing fire,
in trying to frustrate my plan with your deceit.   55
For you, there will be a great pain,
but also for all husbands to come.
For them, as the counterpart to fire, I shall give an evil.
In this counterpart, shall they

all take delight. Her evil competitive spirit,
they shall lovingly embrace."

So said Zeus. And he, the Zeusfather of husbands and gods,
laughed out loud.
He commanded famous Hephaestus
to swiftly   60
mix dry Earth with water,
and to place in it a human voice
and human strength,
and to make its face the likeness of an immortal goddess,
and its shape that of a beautiful and charming virgin.
Then Athena
was to teach it her own special work:
to weave the intricately patterned web.
Then golden Aphrodite
was to pour her own special grace all around its head,   65
the grace that instills a troublesome longing,
a desire that gnaws away at your limbs.
He ordered Hermes,
Zeus' messenger and the Slayer of Argus the monster,
to put inside it
the cunning character of animal intelligence.

So said Zeus.
And they all obeyed Lord Zeus, the son of Cronus.
Without pause,
the famous lame god shaped from the Earth   70
the likeness of a modest virgin,
following the chemical blueprint of the son of Cronus.
The steely-eyed goddess, Athena,
wove the wardrobe web, dressing her and adorning her.
Encircling her, the goddesses,
the Graces (*Charites*) with Lady Persuasion (*Peitho*),
arranged golden jewelry
upon the fleshly surfaces of her body. Encircling her,
the lovely-haired Seasons (*Horai*)
garlanded her hair with the blossoms of spring.   75
Finally, on everything that adorns the skin,
Pallas Athena put her finishing touch.

But then Hermes, Zeus' messenger and
the Slayer of Argus the monster, put into her breast
his cunning character:
wily lies and winning words.
He did this according to the plan of deep-thundering Zeus.
This clever voice that he,
the clever herald of the gods, placed in her,
is the reason why he named this woman   80
Pandora – the "Gift" *for* Whom "Anything Goes."
Also, in her, "anything" a god living on Olympus has
was "gifted" by them to us: *Pandora*
– the "Gift" *into* Whom "Anything Goes."
She is why husbands work for food: a pain.

After Zeus had brought her to completion
(the imposing ruse, invincible to stratagems),
he sent Hermes,
the famous the Slayer of Argus, to Epimetheus.
Hermes, the gods' swift messenger
brought him Pandora as a gift. But Epimetheus   85
had been told by his brother Prometheus
(he whose very name means Fore-Thought)
never to accept a gift from Olympian Zeus,
but instead to send it right back,
so that no evil would come into being for mortals,
the ultimate targets of Zeus' justice.
But Epimetheus (After-Thought)
only thought
about her as evil
after he had married her.

Before that fateful day, the tribes of men,
although living on the ground, still did so   90
separated far apart from all evils,
far apart from any hard labor,
and they had no painful diseases,
the sort which the goddess Death brings for husbands.
Quickly do such distresses
beset mortals now when they grow old.

But on that fateful day, when his wife,
Pandora – the "Gift" *with* Whom "Anything Goes" –
placed her hands on her spouse,
she removed the great lid of Zeus' jar,
everybody now touched   95
by what Zeus had planned for humans:
troublesome toils.
Hope alone remained in the jar.
Hope alone can build an indestructible home.
Hope lingers on the lips.
Hope did not fly outside on that fateful day.
Lingering on the lip of the jar,
with lid replaced, hope abides.

This is all according to the plan
of cloud-gathering Zeus, he who holds the aegis.
But what it decrees is that numberless toils
must now roam among humans.   100
The entire Earth is overrun with evils,
and the sea likewise.
Sometimes diseases creep over humans
during the day, but others at night
bring their evils to mortals, arriving suddenly
and without warning, bearing evil
in silence. Strategic Zeus silences their voices.
So too Pandora's clever voice can
silence any man's rejoinder.
Husbands' proof: there's no escaping the mind of Zeus.   105

If you want me to, I can outline the other half
of this story, the origins of human males.
I can tell it well, because I know what I'm talking about.
Can you train your mind on this?
Do you know how gods and mortal men
came to inhabit the same universe?

The Golden Age

In the beginning, the golden age of men came first.
They were given language. Thus were
they made human, by the immortals
who have palaces on Olympus.   110
These men lived in the time of Cronus,
when he had become king over the Sky.
These men lived like gods,
because their competitive spirit was untroubled,
untouched by work and woe.
None of the decay that belongs to
old age assailed them.
Their arms and legs stayed the same always.
All they did was take pleasure in festivities.
No evil was in sight anywhere.   115
When they died,
it was simply like falling asleep. Nothing ignoble
marked their lives. The land, always fruitful,
never ceased from producing a harvest
effortlessly, without work. With plenty everywhere,
no envy was provoked. All their
tasks they performed voluntarily,
leisure distributed equally among the noble citizenry.
From their wealth, they gave many animals,
dear to the blessed gods in sacrifice.   120

But the golden age still died, being mortal not divine.
And after the Earth received them,
they became bodiless Angels (*daimones*).
These are the noble Angels we talk about
who roam above the ground. Warding off evil,
they are the watchers over mortal humans.
They keep close watch
over legal disputes and merciless deeds.
Clothed in nothing but air,
they stalk the land everywhere.   125
They can make you wealthy.
As nobles, they have this royal prerogative.

The Silver Age

The second age came after,
and it was much worse.
This silver age of men was made by the immortals
who have palaces on Olympus.
Neither in body nor mind
did they resemble the golden age.
For one hundred years,
each child stayed with its mother.   130
For one hundred years, she had to raise it,
fussing over it at home, a big dumb child.
Then when it passed puberty,
that measure of youthful prime,
it didn't live much longer.
Sufferings were brought on
because of their deeply ingrained,
habitually adolescent stupidity. Reckless violence
could not be restrained between them.
As for service to the immortals,   135
they were unwilling to give it.
They offered no sacrifice on the altars of the blessed.
But sacred law decrees that humans offer sacrifice,
as is our custom. Therefore Zeus,
the son of Cronus, in a just anger, made them disappear.
They refused to give honors

to the blessed gods who hold Olympus.
And for that reason they had to die.

So the silver age passed away.
And after the Earth received them,   140
they were called by mortals the Blessed Ones,
our name for those under the ground.
They may have come second,
but nonetheless honor still attends them.

The Bronze Age

Father Zeus then made the third age of humans,
the creatures to whom he gives language.
This bronze age of men
he made completely different from the silver age.
From the ash tree, the spear is made.
So too was the bronze age, terrible and mighty.   145
They cared for nothing but grievous deeds of War (*Ares*)
and lawless violence. No bread
did they eat: farming was not for them.
Their competitive spirit, although steel-willed,
was completely uncivilized.
Their mighty power made their hands invincible.
Backing up their fists were thick arms
growing from their shoulders like tree trunks.
At war, they used bronze armaments.
At leisure, they rested in houses of bronze.   150
Their only occupation was working with bronze.
Iron was unknown and didn't exist yet.
But bronze conquered bronze.
Killed off by their own hands,
they journeyed down into Hades' wide embrace,
cold and dark. What do we call them?
Nobody remembers their names.
Formerly their fists pounded out their fame. But then
dark death throttled them,
and so they departed from the sunny spotlight.   155

The Heroic Age

So the bronze age passed away.
But after the Earth received them,
there was then still another. A fourth age of men,
who turned instead to agriculture,
was made by Zeus, son of Cronus.
Superior to the bronze age, they were more just.
This was the divine age of heroic men.
These heroes, from their parentage, we call
the Demigods. Their age came just before ours,
before we overran boundless Earth.   160

Some of these heroes died
in evil war and horrible combat.
Some died at seven-gated Thebes,
Cadmus' portion of the Earth,
destroyed by the fighting
over Oedipus' flocks.
Others died when by ships
they had crossed over the great gulf of seawater
to Troy, to fight for Helen
and her beautiful hair.   165
It was there that the finality of death
wrapped itself around some of them.

But for half of the heroic humans,
sufficient livelihood, and a place to live, was given to
them by the Zeusfather, the son of Cronus,
when he settled them at the ends of the Earth.
With their competitive spirit untroubled,
they dwell there   170
on the Isles of the Blessed,
beachfront to deep-eddying Ocean.
They are the blessed heroes.
For them, honey-sweet fruit
the fertile soil yields in harvest
three times a year.

The Iron Age

Then yet another age, the fifth age of Men,
was established by Zeus,
that long-term thinker.
I wish that I did not live among the fifth age of Men.
Better to have died before,
or to be born after.   175
This is now the iron age.
Neither in daytime,
nor at nighttime,
does pain and distress ever cease
wearing us down.
The gods have given us difficult things that consume our care.
But even so, for this age,
noble things will be mixed in with the bad.

The Apocalypse

Still, Zeus will destroy this age of humans,
the creatures to whom he gives language,   180
if ever at birth they show gray around the temples.
But we are not born wise. His plan is:

Fathers do not agree with sons.
Sons do not agree with fathers.
Neither does a foreigner with a local.
Nor does one pupil with another pupil.
And siblings shall always be rivals.
(Only once were they not, back in the golden age.)
They shall always be quick
to dishonor their aging parents.   185
They shall always find fault with them,
speaking painful words.
Do these fools not know about
the retribution of the gods? Is that why they do not
make repayment to their aging parents
for bringing them up?

Justice for them is nothing but the fist.
And so one man destroys another man's city.
The man keeping his oath shall never be thanked.
No thanks for the just man,   190
no thanks for the good man.
Better to be doers of evil deeds and lawless violence.
Such men shall always be praised by men.
But if justice lies in the fist, then shameless
is what they shall always be.
The evil man will harm the better man,
speaking his twisted stories,
which he will then seal with an oath.
Every wretched human being,
envy accompanies.   195
Bringing discord,
bringing glee over misfortune,
bringing dirty looks,
envy accompanies.

Envy sends off to Olympus,
away from the wide-pathed ground,
the goddesses whose beautiful skin
is veiled in white robes.
Envy makes them abandon humans,
to seek instead the company of immortals.
Envy drives out Reverence (*Aidos*)
and Righteous Anger (*Nemesis*). Left behind are   200
the toilsome troubles that mar mortal humans.
Without the goddesses, evil is unchecked.

CHAPTER 4: *Hawk and Nightingale*

One fable says it all, and it speaks to kings.
(Disclaimer: our own are wise, of course.)

The hawk addressed the nightingale,
as he held her speckled neck
grasped in his claws,
carrying her high up,
through the clouds.
She, pierced by his hooked talons,
was crying out pitifully in song,   205
shedding tears.
He, who had overpowered her,
blurted out wise advice:

"O boo hoo! What are you crying for?
You are in the grip of someone much stronger.
Nobody cares how well you sing.
You must go wherever I lead you.
If dinner I want,
on you I shall feast,
or else you I'll release.
Anyone who wants
to oppose the stronger
is stupid.   210
Not only is he a loser,
but he compounds his loss
with pain and disgrace."

So said the swift-winged hawk,
that broad-winged bird
overshadowing the nightingale.

So too this book sings for you now,
how the age of iron,
in iron grip,
holds us with talons.

O brother Perses, do you hear Justice (*Dike*) speaking?
Do not compound your insolence.
Any lawless assault turns out badly for a poor mortal.
Not even a rich noble
will be able to endure its consequences.
Even he will be weighed down by   215
all the retribution coming his way.
Better to take the other road. It's less traveled,
but superior, visiting just actions.
Only Justice can restrain an insolent assault;
only Justice should march off with the prize.
A dumb child learns this lesson by suffering.

Without delay, Oath (*Horcus*) catches up
with anybody's crooked judgments.
With a whoosh, she swooshes in,
if Justice is knocked down, dragged around by men   220
fed by bribes. They pretend to adjudicate sacred laws,
but their judgments are crooked.
She, weeping, attends the city
and the customs of its people.
Clothed in nothing but air,
invisibly she will run up alongside those humans
who thought they expelled her.
They did not dispense a fair deal, so she has evil for them.

They who render,
unto strangers and natives, judgments   225
that are fair,
who do not depart,
on a holiday of wickedness, from what is righteous,
for them
their city shall flourish,
and their people prosper within it.
Peace (*Eirene*) shall reign in their corner of the Earth,

nourishing their children.
Never painful war shall Zeus put on them.
He, a long-range thinker, pays tribute to such.

Never is Famine (*Limos*) the follow-up
for men whose judgments are fair.   230
Never do they taste Ruin (*Ate*).
In good cheer instead, they distribute the meat and drink
from their own fields. The Earth brings them
a more than sufficient livelihood: the oaks
on the mountains send forth acorns
on all their branches, and bees swarm in their trunks,
and the wooly sheep
are thick with fleece.

Always shall the women give birth
to children befitting for their fathers.   235
Forever and ever shall the good be teeming.
No need to go abroad
on ships, because in their own fertile land
is abundance of seed.

But for those keen on insolent assault
and merciless deeds,
that long-range thinker, Zeus,
the son Cronus, has decreed Justice.
Most of the time, an evil man's entire city
suffers the punishment   240
paid to the transgressor,
for the reckless deeds he devised.
The son of Cronus applies great pain to them.
From the sky comes
Famine (*Limos*) linked with Plague (*Loimos*).
And the people slowly perish.

Never after shall the women give birth.
Their homes are emptied
in accordance with the designs of Olympian Zeus.
But sometimes he does this   245
by wiping out their whole army,

or by letting their city wall be breached.
Sometimes the son of Cronus
simply plucks their ships off the Sea.

O kings, even you
yourselves can understand
this (invisible taloned) Justice:
it is said that the immortals are near
to us humans,
when by crooked judgments   250
we grind each other down,
taking no heed of the gods' divine vengeance.
The ground can nourish many,
and thirty thousand Angels of the golden age roam over it.
For mortal humans,
Zeus made them the immortal watchers.
They keep close watch
over legal disputes and merciless deeds.
Clothed in nothing but air,
they stalk the land everywhere.   255

Justice, she is a virgin,
sprung from her father, Zeus.
Among the gods who hold Olympus,
she is noble and venerable.
If anyone harms her,
taking her lightly with crooked behavior,
without delay she ascends the throne
next to her father, Zeus, the son of Cronus.
She sings to him of the unjust human mind.
She sings of the atonement   260
the country people pay for their reckless kings.
She sings of their ruinous plans
by which they turned from her,
by which they rendered their judgments crookedly.

O kings, watch out for these things.
Make your judgments straight and fair,
you who have fed on bribes.
Give up entirely your crooked judgments.

He who causes evils for another man,
causes evils for himself.   265
The evil plan is
most evil for he who planned it.
The eye of Zeus sees all.
The mind of Zeus knows all.
If he wishes, he can examine us right now.
Not hidden from him
is that brand of justice a city hammers out
behind closed doors in back rooms.

As for me, why would I myself want
to stand out among human beings as just?   270
Or why would my son?
It is obviously bad to be a just man, since
the more unjust you are, the more will you get,
at least when the judge's verdict arrives.
Zeus is full of stratagems, but I have no hope:
not even he can talk them into a just deal.

O my brother, Perses,
take these things to heart.
Listen to Justice
and forget all use of force.   275
The son of Cronus
has ordained for humans this law:

Fish and beasts
and winged birds
may eat each another,
because Justice is not theirs,
since he gave Justice to humans.
Justice is by far the best thing
that belongs to us. If anyone wishes
to proclaim the things that are just and true,   280
then Zeus, that long-range thinker,
shall bestow on him wealth.
But he who before giving his testimony
willingly swears the oath,
and then lies,

does damage
to Justice,
bringing on incurable harm.
You can see how
the offspring he leaves behind
will be treated like nobodies:
when it comes to justice,
blindness in one generation
makes that family dead to all.
Stronger, better,
is the family of the man
true to his word,
he who keeps his oath. 285

CHAPTER 6: *Work*

Noble things I speak to you, O Perses,
you big dumb child. I have thought this through.
Wickedness is chosen easily.
There is an abundance of attractive
evil deeds. The road to them is smooth,
and it's a short trip: evil is your neighbor.
Sweat, the immortal gods have decreed that
by sweat we achieve
excellence (*arete*). The path to excellence
is long and steep.   290
It's tough going in the beginning.
But as it approaches the peak,
the tough going is easy,
when you see what you have achieved.

This man is the best of all (*panaristos*):
he who, when he thinks about all things,
thinks best, by careful deliberation,
mulling the possible outcomes and which is better.
And noble is the man who heeds the advice
spoken by that kind of man.   295
But he who does not deliberate on his own,
or who does not listen to the man who can
(thereby informing his competitive spirit),
is the man who is worthless to all.

I hope that you, at least,
will always remember our recommendation: *work!*
O my brother, Perses,
you came from a noble family. But if you would
make Famine your enemy, then
make Demeter fall in love with you.   300
A modest goddess, with blossoms in her hair,
she wants your granary full, to live off it.
But Famine is the companion, forever and always,
for the man who shirks work.

Gods and men feel righteous anger
at the man who without working
gets his livelihood. That man's temperament
calls to mind the drones who have no sting,
who without working gorge themselves
on what the honeybees labored for: 305
the only thing they like is eating.
But you should like hard work. Not too much,
not too little. Just do the right amount,
so your granary gets its full seasonal livelihood.

If they work, then men can multiply their flocks,
and abound in wealth.
If they work, then men do become loved,
much more loved, by the immortals.
If they work, then men are even lovable
to other men. Don't we all despise the lazy?   310
There is no disgrace in work.
Idleness is the real disgrace. Do you doubt it? Then
do some work, and you will quickly see:
the idle man envies you, as you
grow rich. Excellence and glory are enviable,
but they come from working for wealth.

No matter what luck your guardian Angel may bring,
work is better than luck.
It is mindless to focus your competitive spirit
on the possessions of others. Turn to   315
your own task. That's all I ask.
A sufficient livelihood for yourself is your only real care.

Reverence is what the needy man has.
Indeed, he may revere wealth! But this is not good.
Reverence: there is more than one kind.
That kind does great harm to men. But there is a
reverence, earned in poverty, which can be a benefit.
This kind eschews arrogant wealth.

CHAPTER 7: *Success*

Don't get your property by theft.
Far better for you to get it as a gift, from the gods. 320
Even if someone, by the force of the fist,
can seize great wealth, watch out.
Even if someone can plunder, by using only his tongue,
watch out (and I know this often
happens, because many times do dreams of big profits
trick people into stupidity).
Watch how poor, reverent humility can turn into
irreverent audacity to get rich
quickly.
That's how the gods blind a man, turn him into nobody,
and empty his home
easily. 325
Wealth may stay only for a short time with a man.
Just watch them lose it all
foolishly.

You want to see dumb?
Look at he who mistreats the suppliant, mistreats the foreigner.
Look at he who climbs up
into his brother's bed
for a clandestine affair with his wife.
Is there ever a fitting season for adultery? 330
Look at he who mindlessly abuses
orphaned children.
Look at he who, when his aging father
has just entered the worst part of old age,
quarrels with him,
assaulting him with cruel words.
Indeed, this makes Zeus himself indignant.
And so the outcome
that Zeus ordains for these unjust deeds is
payment in full, his price as cruel as the crime.

You need to keep your competitive spirit
far away from these mindless deeds. 335
With all of your strength,
offer sacrifices to the immortal gods instead. Make your spirit
pure and clean: burn the thighbones
wrapped up in their fat.
Appease the gods sometimes with libations,
or at other times with burnt offerings.
Do both before you go to bed and also
when the holy light of dawn awakens you.
As a result, your heart will be gentle,
and your competitive spirit, gracious. Sacrifice 340
leads to success: you'll be able to buy up the land of others.
You won't have to sell yours.

Leave your enemies alone. The upside?
You only have to invite your friends to dinner.
The one you really need to invite
is the one who lives closest to you: your neighbor.
If some kind of danger is stalking the countryside,
then neighbors come running
in their bedclothes. But your brother-in-law
will take his time getting dressed. 345
A bad neighbor is a huge pain,
but a good one is an even bigger help.
He who is known as a good neighbor:
that blameless reputation is no small honor.
If a single ox dies, who doesn't blame it on his bad neighbor?
All bad sticks to the bad.
Don't borrow too much from your neighbor.
Pay it all back. A little more if you can. 350
Then later, when you really need a favor,
you'll be able to count on him. Besides,
it's evil to profit at another's expense.
Don't do it. Evil profits will screw *you* the most.

Pay friendliness back with friendliness.
If they came over to see you, go visit them next.
Make sure you give to them who gave to you.
They deserve generosity. The stingy don't.

Givers receive more than they give.
Freeloaders miss out on far more than they get.   355
Generosity is good. Greed is evil.
Death's gift for the greedy: death will make a killing.
To give willingly,
even at great expense, is the only way
to be cheerful when giving.
Placate your competitive spirit with this pleasure.
To yield to shamelessness,
to grab it all for yourself,
even if all you can grasp at are nickels and dimes,
is to be stuck with your own cold heart.   360

If you really want to add to what you have,
then here's the only surefire way to profit and
defend against an outbreak of Famine:
little by little, slowly but surely, store up food.
Add small amounts often. Do it frequently.
Soon enough a big stockpile will be the result.
Whatever is stored up in his home
does not trouble a man.
A stockpile in the home is better
than one outside: trouble lurks outdoors.   365

Noble it is to choose the best present option.
Your competitive spirit is pained
only if you want to gain something not present.
I urge you to rethink those obsessions.
Have as much as you want
from the top of the just-opened jar, or when you hit its bottom.
Just control yourself in between.
You're no hero suddenly finding self-control at the end.

Greed is all around. Even if friends and family
work for you, agree on the salary first.   370
Do it with a smile, but even if he's your brother,
you must get a witness to the agreement.
Trust and misplaced trust: the whole story
of how men are ruined, from beginning to end.

Don't let a woman's shapely bottom
change your mind when you're negotiating a deal.
She'll bombard you with flattery,
but she doesn't really want you: she wants your farm.
If you want to trust women,
you may as well make deals with thieves too. 375

Even if you have only one son, that'll be enough.
It only takes one to inherit the home.
One is enough to sustain the wealth.
It only takes one to multiply what's stored indoors.
But if you have more than one,
may you live to an old age, so you may enjoy this sight:
the vast wealth multiplied by even more.
Zeus can easily bestow it, since
where there are more sons to care for an estate,
all the more can it increase. 380

If your competitive spirit has put a longing
into your heart for wealth, then do it this way:
work for it. Work added to work:
that's the best success, the only real compound interest.

CHAPTER 8: *The Farming Custom* (Nomos)

The Pleiades are the daughters of Atlas.
They rise in early May, before sunrise: summer
begins. Reap your harvest then.
But when they set, in late October, plow and sow then.
At the end of spring, for forty days and forty nights,
the Pleiades are hidden,   385
rising after sunrise, setting before sunset.
But in summer they appear again. And then
the year unwinds, until they set at October's sunrise.
You sharpen your sickle then.
This is the custom of the plains.
This is the custom for those who dwell near the sea.
This is the custom for those who live in the mountain glens,
in fertile land far
from the wave-whipped sea.
The Pleiades hold all the Earth with this cosmic custom.   390

Wherever you dwell, the custom is:
roll up your sleeves and sow,
roll up your sleeves and plow,
roll up your sleeves and reap.
If you want it all, then get to work.
Patience: Demeter's harvest only comes in due season.
Work daily so that each crop
may grow in due time. Otherwise, the time will come,
and your field will be empty.
You'll have to go begging at other men's houses.
What have you achieved? *Nothing.*   395

So now do you come to me. You've done *nothing.*
And so I will give you *nothing.*
One more cup of *nothing* is all I will loan you,
Perses, you dumb child! You must work
the work that the gods have marked out
for us humans.

Otherwise your competitive spirit will choke on this:
one day, with wife and children,
you go beg your livelihood from the neighbors,
but that day they give you *nothing*.   400

Perhaps two or three times you will get lucky
and get fed. Then they'll get sick of you.
Keep it up, and soon you will not succeed.
Your sob story will fall on deaf ears.
Your usual story will soon be useless.
So here's a better custom for you:
stay out of debt
and don't go hungry.

First things first: get a house, get a woman,
get an ox for the plow. Avoid the wily   405
tarts hunting for husbands.
You are shopping for a worker. She'll follow the oxen
and sow the seed. And at home she'll make ready
anything that you need.
Then you won't have to ask another man for help.
When you need it, he could refuse you.
You could lose the whole season. All your work up until then?
Without her, wasted.

Never procrastinate.
Never say you'll do it tomorrow or the next day.   410
Slow workers
never fill their barns.
Neither do procrastinators.
Diligence does the job.
The procrastinating man acquires the work of his hands:
nothing but delusions.

CHAPTER 9: *Autumn's Plow*

The time will come
when the sharp might of the sun stops
making you feel hot and sweaty.
Autumnal rains   415
will be sent by Zeus.
Then mortal flesh
feels refreshed.
This will be when the Dog Star, Sirius,
over the heads of sleeping humans,
humans weighted with cares, rises earlier.
It'll travel only a little while by day.
It'll spend most of its time moving by night.

At that time, wood drops its leaves to the ground.
It stops sprouting.   420
At that time, the wood you cut with your ax
is least likely to worm.
This then is the time to remember: *cut timber*.
This is the season for wood work.

Cut a mortar and pestle,
for grinding the grain.
Cut an axle big enough for a broad cart,
able to carry much, to and from the field.
Cut enough to make a mallet,
for breaking up the clods of earth.   425
Cut the rims and spokes for big wheels,
big enough for a big wagon.
Cut curved pieces, for the plow.
But bring home the piece for the plow beam
when you can find it. You'll have to look
on the mountain or in the meadows
for one of holm oak. That's the strongest wood
for oxen to plow with.
The carpenter, Athena's handyman,

can fix it for you into the share beam. 430
He'll bolt it on with pegs
and fasten it to the pole beam.

At home you should always have
two plows ready for work:
one single-pieced, the other jointed.
This is the better way to prepare to plow.
What if you break one of them?
You can hitch the oxen to the other.
Poles of laurel or elm
are least likely to be eaten by worms. 435
But make the share beam of oak
and the plow beam of holm oak. Then get two oxen.

Get bulls nine years old.
Then their strength is not all used up.
They are in the prime of their youth.
That's when they are best for work.
They won't put up a struggle.
You don't want them in the furrow, breaking
the plow, leaving the work unfinished. 440

The best man to follow behind them
is a fit forty-year-old. (Guess who I'm talking about?
Me!) Be sure you feed him a big meal.
Good food, good mood.
Mature, this man will focus on his work.
He needs to drive a straight furrow.
Mature, he won't be looking around
to see what's going on elsewhere. He will focus
his competitive spirit only on his work.
No young buck can ever be his match. 445
Mature, he knows best how to sow the seed.
He doesn't double up the seed, wasting it.
The younger man always gets distracted by his peers.
Young and dumb! Wasting time!

The time will come
when you hear the voice of the cranes.
Flying in the clouds above,
they move in their southward migration.
This is the sign for you to plow, *now*.
It is also the sign that the season   450
of winter rain approaches. The heart saddens at this sound
only for the man with no oxen!

At that time, feed the curved horned oxen
you have, until then, kept ready indoors. True,
preparation is not easy! Others find it easy to ask:
"Loan me your oxen and your wagon?"
But you can be just as ready with your refusal:
"Sorry, they are busy with my work."

People are lazy dreamers.
They think a wagon need not be built until it is needed.   455
They think like dumb children!
Is not a wagon assembled from a hundred pieces? Is that
really a simple, one-day task? No! Plan ahead.
What's needed isn't lying around at home.

When the time to plow has come,
a time obvious to all mortal men (prepared or not),
then, more than ever, it's time
not to be wasting your time. You and your helpers
must plow, plow, plow, now the season has come.
In wet weather or dry weather,   460
wake up early and do the work.
How else can a land reach its full yield?

Plow the fallow land in the spring.
Even fallow land plowed in the summer will be fine.
Sow the fallow land,
once the soil has been lightly turned by the plow.
Always keep half your land fallow.
Then you can feed your children safely all year.

Make a prayer to Zeus, the protector of the Earth,
and to holy mother Demeter.   465
Ask them to make Demeter's sacred grain
grow to its fullest.
Pray when you start to plow.
And as you grip the plow in your hand, keep praying.
As you smack the backs of the oxen,
keep praying.
As they pull on the pole bar with their yoke straps,
pray. And get human help too!

A little helper should follow you,
working a tool to cover the sown seed.   470
You can't keep the birds away, unless you hide the seed.
All human mortals may attest:
good management brings out the best.
Bad management brings out the worst.
Plow piously, and plow wisely.
Then your grain will grow full and heavy,
since it is Olympian Zeus himself
who decrees fulfillment for a noble effort.

At harvest time, you will cheerfully
brush the cobwebs from your storage bins.   475
Then will you fill your storeroom,
and draw food from it, whenever you need it.
You will have plenty to eat, right up until springtime.
You won't have to look
longingly at others. No, it is the other man
who will come begging to you in his need.

You want to be lazy like him? Go ahead,
wait until winter solstice before you plow!
Your best land will yield only a handful of grain:
so little you can reap it reclining,   480
so short that you can harvest it
lying down in the dust.

Oh well, bind the grain with a fancy bow!
Won't that still delight you?
Carry it in a pricey handbag!
Isn't it style alone that earns cheers?

Remember, it's only Zeus who wears the aegis.
And his mind changes.
He thinks differently
at different times. It is difficult for mortal men
to understand it. So don't presume
your prosperity! Still, even if you do get lazy,
and sow too late, Zeus may give   485
a second chance to you. The song of the cuckoo
will ring out in spring
from behind the leaves of the oak tree.
Then, when the song is making hearts glad
all over the boundless Earth, watch if Zeus
sends rain on the third day. If it does not cease
until rain fills the height of an ox's
hoof – no more, no less – then he who plows late
just got lucky. Zeus may very well grant him
a greater yield than the early plow.   490

Your competitive spirit needs
to store up all this advice. Do not forget
as you watch for the arrival of bright spring.
Look for her season of forgiving rains.

CHAPTER 10: *Winter's Wind*

Don't crowd into the blacksmith's shop,
seeking its heat with everybody else
in wintertime.
Sure, the bitter cold keeps men from
working outside.
But why not work hard at home inside?   495
Otherwise bad winter may overtake you.
And you'll be helpless if
poverty makes you frostbitten
and starving to death.

The only thing for a lazy man to feed on
is vain hopes. He has no livelihood.
All that his competitive spirit can achieve is
to be the best at bitter complaints.
The needy man knows
no good hope.   500
He sits around. He's a big talker.
But he has more dreams than income.

This is why, in the middle of summer,
you must be wise. Command your workers:
"Summer's warmth will not always be here.
Build now a safe shelter for winter."

The worst month of winter
has days that freeze the ass
of even an ox. This is when
you must avoid the cruel wind chill   505
of Boreas, the North Wind,
who blasts across the Earth.
He travels down over horse-breeding Thrace,
crosses the open sea,
whips up its waters,
and then makes Earth and her forests scream.

Tall oak trees, topped with leaves,
sturdy fir trees, topped with green,
they all fall down before him,
swept down, crashing   510
on the mountainside.
He roars through the forests,
making even the wildest animals shiver.
Tails between their legs, they cower before him.
It doesn't matter if their hides
have fur. His bitter blast
blows through
even the thickest of skins.

He slices right through the hide of an ox.
It is no defense against him.   515
He assaults the shaggy goat's pile of hair.
Only a sheep's fleece stands a chance.
Sheep wool is so thick,
usually Boreas is unable to pierce it.
So then, what about an old man?
Well, what do you think? Boreas spins him like a wheel.

But here's a comforting thought:
he cannot touch the tender skin of a young girl
who stays safe inside
her dear mother's home.   520
She does not yet know
the ways of golden Aphrodite.
Even so, she warmly bathes her soft limbs.
Having dried, she anoints her body
with fragrant oil. Then she lies down
in the inmost room. There she waits, expectantly.

Meanwhile, at the bottom of the sea,
the boneless octopus can only feed on himself.
In winter, his ocean home turns bleak,
without warmth, and he has no option left.   525
The sun used to show him where he could feed,
but now it has departed. Instead,
the sun roams vigorously over Africa,

keeping the dark-skinned peoples warm.
As for Greece, in winter,
the sun shines on us only reluctantly.

Meanwhile, in the forest,
the creatures, horned and unhorned alike,
whimper as their teeth chatter.
When Boreas blows, they bolt through the trees   530
looking for shelter. One care,
and one care only, do they have:
to find protection in some hiding place,
to be safe
within the hollow of a rocky cave.
But they move like an old man with a cane:
bent over by nature's assault,
the head can only look down.
When winter thus descends,
one wanders in the falling white, looking for escape.   535

But if you plan on going outside,
then I say cover up your skin with layers.
Wear a soft and flexible outer coat,
but wear inner clothing over your body's full length.
Make sure the fabric is double-woven,
to be durable and resistant to the cold.
You will know you have clothed yourself right
if not one of your hairs can move.
Give no room on your skin for them
to bristle and shiver, standing on end.   540

Cover your feet well, with good boots that fit.
On their outsides, you want the hide
of a slaughtered ox and,
on their insides, a thick felt lining.
When winter's frosty season arrives,
then make use of ox's sinew to
sew together some skins from newborn goats.
Put this on your back. You'll find
it'll keep the rain off.
Up on top, put on your head   545

a fitted cap, made of felt.
If fitted right, it'll keep your ears dry.

Boreas descends at daybreak,
and attacks the morning with his chill.
But still, dawn's mist spreads itself
out over the Earth. It falls from starry Sky
as a blessing,
down upon the wheat-bearing fields.
This mist has its source
in rivers that flow forever.   550

Sometimes a windstorm
raises this mist on high, over the Earth. If so,
in evening, it may turn to rain.
Sometimes it blows as the wet wind
Boreas sends from Thrace.
Then its onslaught even pushes aside thick clouds.
Get your work done and get home
before Boreas chooses either of these evening options.
Do not let the dark wetness from the sky
envelop you.   555
It'll soak your skin
and soak your clothes.

Indeed, the worst month of winter
is very harsh. So why go outside to meet him?
He greets you only with chilly Boreas.
He is harsh on flocks, and harsh on humans.
Since not much work can be done outside,
oxen need only half of their usual food ration.
But console yourself by taking a little more than half.
The nights are long and cold.   560

Exercise caution in winter,
just as I have advised. Then when the year is ended,
when the days are again
as long as the nights, then again
will Earth, the mother of all, yield for us
all of her abundant fruits.

CHAPTER 11: *Spring's Swallow and Summer's Wine*

After the winter solstice,
Zeus decrees that sixty more
days of winter will follow.
Then will the star   565
Arcturus rise up
from the sacred waters of Ocean.
Marking the new season,
it will shine brightly at dusk.
Then the swallow, King Pandion's daughter,
will sound to humans her song of woe.
She laments her tragic rape,
but now in metamorphosis, sings the beginning of spring.

Prune the vines
before the swallow sings, for this is best.   570
But when the snail, up from the earth,
carrying his house on his back, crawls up plants
(as if in flight from the Pleiades!), then cease
the hoeing in your vineyards.
Tend instead to harvest: sharpen your sickles,
and summon your workers.

You can't hide in the shade,
or sleep past dawn,
when the harvest time arrives.
True, the sun beats down on your hot skin.   575
That's why you have to make haste.
How else will you bring home the harvest,
unless you get up early? Get the jump on the day's heat,
and secure your livelihood.

Get a third of your work
done at dawn.
Work at dawn, and you are on the way.
Work at dawn, and the job gets done.

When the light of dawn appears,
what can you see?   580
See how she lights the way of many on the right path.
See how she yokes many oxen.

But when summer comes,
the golden thistle will flower. The cicada will sing out
from his perch in the tree.
He will chirp his song
by beating his wings.
Who else cares to sing in this wearisome heat?
In summertime, goats grow most fat,
and wine tastes most sweet.   585
Women are most hot and bothered,
and men are too tired to put up a fight.

In the dog days of summer,
the star Sirius weakens heads and wobbles knees.
Skin shrivels dry in the heat.
So what better time is there for me
to find a shady retreat? On a cool rock,
I shall drink the finest Bibline wine.
For an appetizer, I shall eat cheese bread,
dipped in goat's milk.   590
Then shall I feast on steak, on the juiciest cut
from the most expensive cow, with roast
baby goat's meat on the side. I'll wash it all down
with that fine red wine, and keep on
sipping it as I sit in the shade. And then,
when full of food and wine,
my heart is happy …
I shall turn my head to face west,
towards the refreshing Zephyr wind, and smile.
Then shall I make my prayer, and pour out
pure water, taken from a living spring,   595
in three libation offerings. But the fourth libation
will seal my prayer with that holy wine.

But then in July, you must summon
your workers again, to winnow the sacred grain

of Demeter, when mighty Orion
first appears in the sky.
You will need a level threshing floor
in a well-ventilated place.
Measure out the grain
as you store it in your jars. Then,   600
when your livelihood is safe and secure,
stored up inside your house,
you may dismiss your workers.
You may replace them now with just
a servant girl. But make sure she has no children.
Why hire a screaming headache?

At this time, you also need a guard dog.
Get one with sharp teeth. Feed him well.
If you fail to take my advice,
then you will lose your grain to a thief in the night.   605

And did you stock up on hay and fodder?
You will need enough to feed
your oxen and your mules. Did you do this
before dismissing your workers?
It'll be their last task. Then they may rest
their weary knees, as oxen now unyoked.

In September, Orion and Sirius arrive
in the middle of
the sky, and rosy-fingered Dawn
sees Arcturus rising.   610
This is the time to carry home, from the vine,
the clusters of grapes. Perses, do you see?
Pruned before the swallow sang,
it now rewards a man's prudence. Dry the grapes
in sunlight for ten days. Cool them in shade
for five days. On day six, press into jars
the juicy gifts. Dionysus is joyful when the best wine
is won thus, by practical wisdom.

By November, the Pleiades
and the Hyades and mighty Orion   615
will have set. Do you remember what to do now?
Yes, time again to plow.
Thus wind the seasons. The constellations
of spring and summer turn under the ground.

CHAPTER 12: *The Risky Sea*

Maybe you'll harvest so much grain,
you think of sailing the stormy sea to sell it.
But don't be like the Pleiades.
They dip into the dark sea, to escape
from mighty Orion, in late October,
during plowing season!   620
Not only that, the wild windblasts
are then at their worst.
No, at that time ships have no business
being on the wine-dark sea.
Are you listening to me? Stay home
and do farm work. Work the plow.

If you have a ship, that is the time
to place her in dry dock. Pack stones closely around.
This will be her defense, immobile,
when the wet winds seek to knock her down.   625
Keep her drain hole open, otherwise
the rain will build up, and rot her insides out.
Store in your home
all the sailing gear.
Stack up neatly the oars, because you need
reliable wings for your ship. And
in this time, the ship's rudder has no use,
except as a trophy above your fireplace.
Perses, do you understand yet?

Everything has a proper season, especially sailing.   630
If you do set sail in a swift ship over the waters,
then please be smart enough to stow
an appropriate cargo. There is no sense in
transporting yourself from profit into loss.
Perses, you big dumb child!
Did you not learn from our own father's experience?
He too, the sailing salesman with a shipload,
chased the dream of living like nobility.

Once upon a time, he even came *here*.
He had to cross a vast expanse of sea.   635
He came down from Aeolian Cyme,
all the way to ascend ass-end Ascra.
He had fled from neither comforts,
nor riches, nor prosperity.
He sailed seeking all that:
refuge from Zeus' evil curse upon men, their poverty.
But then he had to settle here,
near Helicon, in a lousy little town,
Ascra. Crap? Yeah!
Harsh winters. Sweaty summers. Nowhere near noble.   640

So where will you end up, Perses?
Where will you be stuck, if you don't remember
that every deed done, to be done well,
must discern a proper season? Especially sailing!
Wow, look at that fancy little ship!
Oh, wouldn't cargo be safer in a big ugly one?
Wow, look at all the inventory you transport!
The bigger the pile, the bigger your profits!
Oh, won't you be stuck, bankrupted for life,
if the storm winds decide to sink it all?   645

But your competitive spirit
favors the foolish turn, from farming to trading.
Why? You want to escape from your debts.
You take no delight in hunger.
Well then, let me instruct you in moderate deeds.
Let me sing of the loud-roaring sea.

I admit that I am no expert when it comes to sea travel.
What do I know about rich crafts?
Do I look like Helen of Troy?
Never have I ever sailed on a ship across the wide sea.   650
I've only made one short boat trip:
from Aulis to Euboea. Aulis is where the Achaeans
once parked and waited out the storm.

That was when their mighty armada had been
mustered from all over divine Greece.
They sailed off to subdue Troy's beautiful women.

From Aulis I sailed over,
to compete in the games at Chalcis.
In honor of noble Amphidamas,
a great-souled man, his sons   655
had established many great prizes.
May I boast about what happened at Chalcis?
With my song, the *Theogony*, I won first prize.
I was awarded a trophy, a tripod cauldron,
which I took home. I set it up as a monument,
dedicated to the Muses of Helicon, on that
spot by sacred Helicon, where they had breathed into me
a clear-speaking, inspired voice.

I can't number all the bolts in a ship.
But I can number the trips I've made. One!   660
Yet that same one is all the proof you need
to trust my song. I sing of the mind of Zeus,
he who holds the aegis. The Muses themselves
taught me to sing heaven-sent hymns.

Fifty days
after the summer solstice,
the season of summer's most wearisome heat
will be over.
That is the best time for mortals to set sail.
The weather won't smash   665
up your ship and send your sailors drowned
down at the bottom of the sea.
Even so, Poseidon, the Earth Shaker,
might still bring that about.
Even so, Zeus, the king of the immortal gods,
could choose your destruction.
Either good or evil can happen,
when their plans are fulfilled.
But as for the weather then,
steady is the breeze and safe is the sea.   670

You won't have to worry about
whether your swift ship can trust the winds.
So drag it out of dry dock, and drop it in the sea,
filled up with your cargo.

But don't waste time on the trip.
Hasten to get back home again. Don't get caught
at sea when you could be at home
for the season of new wine. That is the season of
autumnal rains and chilly storms.
The south wind, Notus, blows hard then.   675
Zeus sends Notus
to accompany the heavy autumnal rains.
But this stirs the sea into upheaval.
Crossing the open water in those waves is suicide.

There is only one other opportune time
for humans to sail. It is in spring,
when you first see the leaves
sprouting on top of the fig tree.   680
At that time, the shoots are no bigger
than a crow's footprint. The sea is traversable then,
in the spring sailing season.
But I myself do not recommend it.
My competitive spirit
is not stirred by it at all.
At most, you can fit in a quick trip.
More likely, you'll get into trouble on the spring sea.

But why then do humans sail,
even in dangerous times? Is it out of ignorance?   685
The answer is simple:
for wretched mortals, *money is life*.
But waves are death. Aren't they?
Death by drowning is terrible. So take my advice to
keep in mind everything I say,
when you plan your get-rich-quick trip. I say:

Do you really want to gamble
your entire livelihood by placing it inside a fragile ship?
Leave the greater part on land.
Risk only a smaller part at sea.   690
Disaster at sea is a terrible turn of fortune.
Waves are death.
Would you ever take such a risk on land?
Would you load all you own onto your wagon?
It's obvious that is how to break its axle.
Then everything would spill and be spoiled.

This is the lesson: moderate deeds.
Everything done well has discerned a proper season.

CHAPTER 13: *Practical Piety*

There is a proper time.
At that time, bring into your home a wife.   695
You should be thirty years old.
Not much younger,
not much older.
That's the proper age for marriage.

Your future wife? She'll be four years past puberty.
Marry her in the fifth, when she's
eighteen. Be sure to marry a virgin,
a girl open to being schooled in proper behavior.
Indeed, the type you want is
"the girl who lives next door." But you're not getting   700
married to gratify your neighbors.
So scour the neighborhood for just the right girl.

There's no better prize
won by a man than a wife,
as long as she's a *good* wife. If not?
Then there's nothing *worse* than a bad wife.
A bad wife is a parasite. She'll eat her man raw.
She needs no fire; she'll roast even the
strongest man with her words.
She'll wear him down, into old age before his time.   705

Mortal man, avoid such a woman.
And be on guard also to avoid the wrath of the gods
dispensing quarrels. You can't rely on an acquaintance
the same way you can a brother.
But if you wish to cultivate real friendships,
then never be the first to rock the boat. No,
I am not advising you to smooth everything over
with gracious lies. If your friend wrongs
you, being the first to give offense
with a word or deed from a competitive spirit,   710

then remember to stand up for yourself
and pay him back twice as much. But if he asks
you to be his friend again, and intends
to act justly toward you, then
welcome the gesture. Only the petty man
makes it a regular custom to drop old friends
and take up new friends. But I'm not advising you
to censor your heart among friends.

Don't get a reputation,
either as Mr. Popular or as The Misanthrope, 715
or as someone who hangs out with low-lifes,
or who always bad-mouths everyone better.

Don't make fun of the poor man.
Nobody wants to be poor. Sadly, poverty can kill
a man's competitive spirit.
Only the immortal gods can be blamed for such a curse.
Control of the tongue is the best treasure
for humans to possess. Be sparing
with your words. That maximizes their pleasure.
Grace shines best in moderation. 720
If you speak evil words,
then you will soon hear worse ones – about yourself.

Don't be loud and obnoxious at a potluck dinner
where there are many guests you don't know.
The best way to have fun there
is to feast instead on what everyone else has on offer.

Never pour your morning libation
of sparkling wine to Zeus
if you have not first purified the hand
that pours it. All the other immortal gods 725
will also take offense. All the gods
spit a man's impious prayers right back at him.

Do you laugh at piety? Do you think
to bother with rules is silly? Well, do you care to
watch a man take a piss right in broad daylight?

Even in the dark of night, do you want
to come across someone pissing
in the middle of the road? Who do you think cares
to see you exposed? Show some decency.
Nighttime is also blessed by the gods.   730
The pious man practices discretion.
He behaves seasonally. He knows the proper place.
He knows the way
to the restroom.

Indeed, some things are improper.
Don't go warm your genitals by the fire right after sex.
Who do you think wants to gaze upon that?
Hestia, the virgin goddess of the hearth?
And what sort of behavior is proper
for the day of a funeral? Is that the right time   735
to impregnate your wife? Save it for a festival day.
Celebrate the immortals in that way.

Waters are sacred. So never wade into
the eternally flowing water of a lovely river
to make a journey until you have prayed first.
Gaze into the lovely stream as you pray.
Then wash your hands
in the beautiful, clear water.
He who does not purify himself with this gesture
crosses a river wicked and unclean.   740
The gods resent his impiety.
Toward him they allot future punishment.

Do you laugh at piety? Do you think
to bother with rules is silly? Well, what if on a holy
feast day, at your grand dinner party,
one of your guests cuts his fingernails at the table?

While we're on the subject of inappropriate behavior
at a party, don't you think fistfights
will soon erupt if you let your guests
mix their own drinks? An open bar tempts fate.   745

My point is simple. Piety is common sense.
You cut planks all to the same size when you
build houses. But impiety, lawless,
slaps up a home where only birds of ill omen perch.

So say your prayers
before you use water to cook. Say your prayers
before you use water to bathe. Waters are sacred.
Impiety knows not their worth.

Let me paint you a picture of impiety:
a twelve-year-old boy loafing on a gravesite.   750
Is that appropriate? May the gods
rob him of his fertility! Spare us *his* impious progeny.
What about a one-year-old baby
playing on a tombstone?
No excuse. Blame his parents.
It's the same as if a man were to bathe
using the water that a woman had just bathed in.
Do you see? Impurity comes from
inappropriate mixing, two things unseasonably mixed.
There is a price to be paid for that.
So do not mock men who make burnt offerings   755
to atone for their sins. God has ceased
directing wrath at them. He'll now direct it at *you*.
The impious man's crimes
are not simply flushed out to sea like piss down a toilet.
The impious man is pissing
in everybody's drinking water. Don't be that man.
You wouldn't take a dump in the sink.
So don't dump your impiety where piety purifies.

Piety is practical.
It is how you ward off malicious gossip.   760
Riddle me this:
what is easily acquired,
is lightly passed around
by others, but heavily borne by you,

and very hard to get rid of?
Answer: your reputation.
You can't shake off
your reputation as long as
people will talk. In that way,
reputations are immortals.
But is yours worthy of the gods?

Appendix: The Days

[Note: this appendix to Hesiod's Works, *known as the* Days, *is likely not by Hesiod.]*

Be prudent. Some days sent by Zeus
are more auspicious than others.   765
Instruct your workers, who pay attention to days.
The thirtieth, the last day of the month,
is when you have their attention:
on payday, review their performance.

Let me report now about the days sent by Zeus,
who is always full of stratagems,
telling you what men say they have been able to discern
about what the god intends.

Sacred are the first, the fourth,
and the seventh days of the month.   770
On the seventh day Leto gave birth
to Apollo of the golden sword.
The eighth and the ninth days
also fall within the first phase of the month,
when the moon is waxing.
These two days are good for mortals to do work.

The eleventh and twelfth days of the month
are also excellent for doing work,
hard work like shearing sheep
or bringing in the fruits of the harvest.   775
But of these two, the twelfth day

is naturally better than the eleventh day. On it
you will see the spider swinging in the air
and spinning her web in a full day's work.
You will also see the wise ant
heaping up her pile.
It's a perfect day, then, for a woman
to set up her loom and get on with her work.

Avoid sowing on the thirteenth day
in the first phase of the month,   780
when the moon is waxing. But you will find
that is the best day for transplanting.

The sixth day of the mid-month phase
is a bad day for new plant growth.
But it's a good day for the birth of a son.
It's not a good day for a daughter
to be born on,
or later to be married on.

Neither is the sixth day in the first phase of the month
a good day for daughters.   785
But it's a good day for gelding
your flock's kids and lambs
and for setting up
the sheepfold.
It's a good day for the birth of a son.
But that son will like to taunt others,
tell lies, use flattery,
and be sneaky.

On the eighth day of the month,
geld the boar and the bellowing bull,   790
but geld your hardworking mules
on the twelfth day.

The twentieth day of the month is great.
Men born on it are wise.
They have careful
and critical minds.

And the tenth day is a good day
for the birth of a son. But the fourth day
of the mid-month phase is better for a daughter.
Tend your sheep and horned cattle   795
and your sharp-toothed dog
and hardworking mules on this mid-month day,
stroking them with your hand.
But avoid the heartbreaking troubles
which may come your way on the fourth day
of the month's waxing and waning phases.
That beginning and ending fourth day
can be a very bad day.

But on a fourth day of the month
you can still bring home a bride,   800
as long as the omens of birds tell you
that it is favorable to do so.

Watch out for all fifth days.
They are difficult and dreadful.
On a fifth day, they say,
the Furies were midwifes
at the birth of Oath (*Horcus*).
Strife (*Eris*) bore Oath to be a plague unto perjurers.

On the seventh day of the mid-month phase,
carefully survey your surroundings   805
and cast Demeter's holy grain
upon the level threshing floor.
This is also the day for a carpenter
to cut beams for building houses
or timbers
suitable for building ships.
Then on the fourth day you may
begin to build the tightly fitted ships.

The ninth day of the mid-month phase
gets better in the evening.   810
The ninth day of the first phase,
the month's waxing phase, does no harm to humans.

This is a good day for giving birth,
for a child to be born,
whether male or female.
It can never be a wholly bad day.

Few people know that
the twenty-seventh day of the month is the best
for opening up a wine jar. It's also the best
for putting the yoke on the necks of   815
oxen and mules
and swift-footed horses.
It is also the best for launching
a swift and many-oared ship
into the wine-dark sea.
Indeed, few people name things truly.

On a fourth day open up the wine jar.
The fourth day of the mid-month phase
is the most sacred. Few people know that
the fourth day after the twentieth day   820
is at its best in the morning.
Toward evening, it is not as good.

Such are the days
about which we mortals
who live on the ground
may know something.
All the rest are variable,
evenhanded,
and bring random fortune.
Everybody praises their favorite day.
But few know what they're talking about.
Sometimes a day can be a stepmother.
Sometimes it can be a mother.   825

Happy and blessed is the man
who knows all this lore
about all these days,
but who still does his work
with piety every day,

giving no offense to the immortals.
This man judges truly
what every flight of birds
is aiming at:
deliverance from evil.

Afterword

Eric Voegelin on Hesiod's Poetic "Truth" – Against the Untruth of Society

Excerpted from Eric Voegelin, "Hesiod," chap. 5 in *Collected Works*, vol. 15, *Order and History: Volume II: The World of the Polis* (Columbia, MO: University of Missouri Press, 2000) 195–200. Reprinted with permission of University of Missouri Press.

The creation of philosophy as a symbolic form is the achievement of Hellas. The new form begins to disengage itself from the myth, toward the end of the eighth century, in the work of Hesiod inasmuch as in his *Theogony* the myth is submitted to a conscious intellectual operation, with the purpose of reshaping its symbols in such a manner that a "truth" about order with universal validity will emerge. Metaphysical concepts are incipiently formed, and their formation raises problems that in turn press toward further consistent elaboration. In brief: The speculative reason of the thinker asserts its autonomy against the mythopoetic mode of expression. The pathos of being and existence, which hitherto had expressed itself compactly in the form of the myth, now tends toward a more differentiated mode of expression through the instrument of speculation.

From Myth to Metaphysics

The transition from myth to metaphysics is fraught with problems that science has not yet resolved by far. Still, one can formulate the central issue: that rational speculation, while it can be used within the symbolic forms of both myth and philosophy, is neither the one nor the other.[1] Myth and philosophy, just as myth and revelation, are separated by the leap in being, that is, by the break with the compact experience of cosmic-divine order through the discovery of the transcendent-divine order. The leap in being, however, notwithstanding the radicalism of the event when it occurs, is historically prepared by a variety of modes in which the myth is loosened up and made transparent toward transcendent order. In the Egyptian form of order, the theogonic speculation of the Memphite Theology, the summodeistic speculations of the empire theologians, culminating in the symbolism of Akhenaton, as well as the personal piety of the Amon Hymns, made the cosmological myth so transparent for transcendent being that the resulting for-mulations could be misunderstood by historians as "monotheistic." The carrier of this advance is man inasmuch as his existence under God is real even though it is not yet illuminated by the leap in being. The desire to know the truth of order, which Aristotle recognized as natural to man, is present even where it has to struggle with the compactness of experience and its cosmological expression. In Hellas these preparatory steps toward the leap in being were taken by the "singers." Homer created the present of man, if not under God, at least under the monarchically organized Olympians, and with it the past of memorable deeds and the future of survival in song. Hesiod, to whom the symbolism of existence under the Olympian gods was already given, applied rational speculation to it in his pursuit of truth. The Hesiodian speculation, however, does not belong to the same type as the Egyptian, for the Olympian myth of Homer, to which it applied, was no longer cosmological. The decisive step toward the creation of the historical form had been taken by Homer when he transfigured the Achaean fall into the past of Hellenic society. Unlike the Egyptian speculation, which remained an event within the medium of the cosmological form, the Hesiodian work has its sequel in philosophy because it moves within the mnemosynic form of the singer; the poems of Hesiod are a symbolism *sui generis* inasmuch as they establish a genuinely transitional form between myth and metaphysics. To be sure, since the compact symbols of the myth comprehend shades of experience that escape the differentiated concepts of metaphysics, while the language of metaphysics lends precision to meanings that remain inarticulate in the myth, the units of meaning cannot be simply paired off against each other. Nevertheless, the transition is an intelligible process, because the experiential substratum provided by Homer remains recognizable in its sameness through the change of symbolic forms; and this sameness is most clearly recognizable in the Hesiodian beginnings of the process when, in faltering and stumbling speculation, the symbols of the myth point searchingly toward meanings for which later generations of philosophers will develop a technical vocabulary. The *Theogony* represents such an incipient penetration of the Olympian myth with a speculative intention; and an intelligible line of speculative evolution runs from these beginnings through the Ionian and Italian philosophers to Plato and Aristotle.

The continuity of this evolution was recognized in antiquity. The term *theology*, coined by Plato, was used by Aristotle for designating his *prima philosophia* (the later "metaphysics"): "There are three theoretical philosophies: The mathematical, the physical, and the theological."[2] With a fine sense for historical derivation Aristotle understood the Hesiodian *Theogony* as the first clear step toward philosophical speculation. He was inclined, however, to distinguish Hesiod and his followers as the "early theologizing" from the Ionians as the "early philosophizing" thinkers;[3] and he found the specific trait of the "theologians" in their habit of speculating "mythologically" (*mythikos*).[4] In one of its meanings the new term *theology* was used by Aristotle for designating the form of symbolization, intermediate between myth and philosophy, that we find in Hesiod.[5]

The preliminary characterization of Hesiodian form leads to the question why the myth should have been found wanting as a medium of expression, and what changes in the substratum of experience made speculation appear necessary as a supplementary medium. Fortunately Hesiod himself supplies the answers. His incipient speculation is a response to the experience of social unsettlement.

Hesiod's father came to Boeotia over the sea from the Aeolian Cyme in Asia Minor. The father took to seafaring in order to improve his insufficient livelihood. One of these trips was final. He "left Aeolian Cyme and fled, not from riches and substance but from wretched poverty which Zeus inflicts upon men," and he settled in Boeotia in the miserable village of Ascra, which is "bad in winter, sultry in summer, and good at no time."[6] He found subsistence but no riches. On his death the inheritance was divided between Hesiod and his brother Perses. A not too rosy situation was aggravated by the corruption of the village notables insofar as Perses was able to obtain the larger part through bribing the magistrates.[7] Experience with women also seems to have not been the best, for references to the deadly race of women who are "no help in poverty," who stay at home and let the man work, have an autobiographical ring.[8] By economic status he was a "shepherd of the wilderness," an "ugly shame," a "mere belly."[9] And to make the measure full, the tricky Perses was just involving him in another lawsuit to rob him still further with the help of conniving judges, the princes (*basileis*) of *Works and Days*.[10]

Such hardships will cause a man to reflect on his position in the world and society, as well as on the meaning of an order which on the surface has become doubtful, if reflection be his talent and if the state of civilization furnish him with the means for articulating his thought. Both conditions were fulfilled in the case of Hesiod. The literary form in general, which will be discussed further, was provided by the Homeric poems, and the means of articulation in detail by a wealth of highly developed myths and fables. Moreover, the personal factor, i.e., the will and talent of using these instruments for a reflective penetration of the meaning of order, was certainly present as evidenced by the Hesiodian work; and it was present not only in fact, but also reflectively to the poet's consciousness as a new adventure of man in dealing with problems of order. For the *Theogony* opens with the story of the Heliconian Muses, who appeared to the shepherd Hesiod, endowed him with the staff of the rhapsode, and breathed into him the voice of the singer who celebrates things past and to come. This story in itself was an innovation insofar as the poet stepped out of the anonymity of the older epic and appeared in person, naming himself as the vessel of inspiration. Moreover, the personal appearance was motivated by Hesiod's consciousness of the difference between the inspiration of the older poetry and his own, and even of an opposition to that of Homer. For the Muses, when breathing the voice into Hesiod, informed him that they were quite capable of telling falsehoods (*pseudea*) that sounded like the real thing – apparently a slap at Homer – but that they also knew how to tell the truth (*alethea*) when they chose, and that is what they intended to do in the case of Hesiod.[11] Apparently it was the personal distress of Hesiod, his suffering from injustice, that motivated him to break the older anonymity, to appear as the individual man in opposition to the accepted order, and to pit his knowledge of truth against the untruth of society.

With the speculative penetration of the myth we see the problem of truth developing a gamut of shades. What is the truth of the old myth? What is the source of truth in the philosopher's speculation? What change of meaning does an old myth undergo when it is told as a paradigmatic fable in a context of speculative truth by Hesiod? What kind of truth has a god when he is shaped by Hesiod, as far as we can see, to fit a speculative requirement? What kind of truth have the genealogies of gods invented by Hesiod? These questions run from now on through the history of Greek thought until they come to their head in Plato's struggle with the truth of the old myth to which he opposes the truth of his new myth of the soul, and especially in Plato's much misunderstood invention of a false myth, a "lie" (*pseudos*), by the side of his true myths in the *Republic*.[12] A new kind of truth is the fundamental concern of Hesiod, and the assurance that he is telling "true things" (*etetyma*) recurs in the *Works and Days*.[13]

It is in the light of this concern that we must read the curious passage, in the *Theogony*, on the cathartic effect of articulating the inspired truth. The Muses, and in particular Calliope, attend to the princes and to the singers. When the Muses honor a prince, gracious words will flow from his lips, and his wisdom and judgment will settle great quarrels. When the people are misguided in assembly, he will set matters straight with the ease of his persuasion. And when such a true prince passes through the place of assembly, people will greet him reverently like a god. The cathartic, ordering effect of the prince on the turbulence of the people is paralleled by the rhapsode's effect on the turmoil of the individual soul. When the soul of a man is in sorrow through recent grief, and distress fills his heart with anxiety, he will forget his disturbance when the servant of the Muses sings the glorious deeds of the men of old and of the blessed gods.[14]

The Muses are the daughters of Zeus, of the ordering force of the universe. They transmit the Jovian order to the prince and the singer, for further transmission to the people, as well as to man in his solitude. The Music truth of the prince and the singer that has such cathartic effect is not a piece of true information. It rather is the substance of order asserting itself against the disorder of passion in society and man. Hesiod, thus, distinguishes the three levels of truth and order in God, society, and man that we still can recognize, in their philosophical transformation, in Aristotle's three levels of autarky in God, polis, and man. Moreover, the Muses are the daughters of Zeus from Mnemosyne, from Memory. Zeus fathered them with Mnemosyne when he sought forgetfulness (*lesmosyne*) from ugliness and a rest from his own unruly immortals.[15] Zeus himself, thus, needs an assuaging of his heart, and he finds it in cosmic Memory as the mortals in the memory of their myth. And again we can hear the late echo of the Hesiodian catharsis through Mnemosyne in Plato's anamnesis, especially in the late symbolic form of the *Timaeus* where memory hearkens back to the cosmos for the hints of true order that will overcome the disorder of the age.

ERIC VOEGELIN

NOTES

1 Throughout the present chapter on Hesiod the analysis of the Egyptian "Dynamics of Experience" in *Order and History*, vol. 1, chap. 3, sec. 3, is presupposed.

2 Aristotle *Metaphysics* 6.1026a18f. For the same classification of "theoretical sciences" cf. *Metaphysics* 11.1064ff.

3 *Protoi theologesantes, protoi philosophesantes, Metaphysics* 1.983b29 and 982b11ff.

4 *Metaphysics* 3.1000a9, with special reference to Hesiod as a theologian, and 1000a18. Cf. Werner Jaeger, *The Theology of the Early Greek Philosophers* (London: Oxford University Press, 1947), 9–17.

5 A very important attempt to deal with the intermediate symbolic form of Hesiod was made by Olof Gigon, *Der Ursprung der griechischen Philosophie: Von Hesiod bis Parmenides* (Basel: Schwabe, 1945), especially 36–40. I find myself in agreement with Gigon's analysis as far as it goes but I doubt that this distinction of symbolic means ("Alles wird Person" – "Alles wird zum Gegenstand") is sufficient to cover the problems which in Greek philosophy arise, not from the side of the symbols but from the side of the experiences expressed by their means. The symbolization of transcendent reality as *eidos*, form, in Plato's philosophy, for instance, illustrates the predominance of "Sachanalogie." Nevertheless, the Platonic experience of transcendent being is of importance in itself – and it is closer to the Hesiodian range of experience, with its expression through the personal symbols of the myth, than to the world experience of Ionian philosophers.

6   *Works and Days*, text and trans. by Hugh G. Evelyn-White, Loeb Classical Library (London: Heinemann, 1936), 631–40. Throughout this chapter I am using the translation by Evelyn-White [of both the *Theogony* and the *Works and Days* in his Loeb edition] but take the liberty of making small changes, whenever they seem desirable for sharpening the meaning. Also used were the text of *Hesiodi Carmina*, ed. Aloisius Rzach, 3rd ed. (Leipzig: Teubner, 1913), as well as the following works of interpretation: Ulrich von Wilamowitz-Moellendorf, *Hesiods Erga* (Berlin: Weidmann 1928); Jaeger, *Paideia*, vol. 1; Jaeger, *The Theology of the Early Greek Philosophers*; Friedrich Solmsen, *Hesiod and Aeschylus* (Ithaca, NY: Cornell University Press, 1949); and Frederick J. Teggart, "The Argument of Hesiod's *Works and Days*," *Journal of the History of Ideas* 8 (1947).

7   *Works and Days*, 37ff.

8   *Theogony*, 590ff.

9   Ibid., 26ff.

10   *Works and Days*, 33ff.

11   *Theogony*, 26ff.

12   On the problem of truth and lie in Greek thought cf. Wilhelm Luther, *Wahrheit und Lüge im ältesten Griechentum* (Leipzig: Koehler Ameland, 1935).

13   *Works and Days*, 10.

14   *Theogony*, 75–103.

15   Ibid., 53ff.

About the Translator

C.S. MORRISSEY is a professor of philosophy at Redeemer Pacific College, the Catholic liberal arts college at Trinity Western University in Langley, British Columbia, where he also teaches courses in the Latin language and in Greek and Roman history. He studied Greek and Latin at the University of British Columbia and has taught courses in these languages and in other classical subjects at Simon Fraser University. Morrissey specializes in philosophical theology and his recent focus has been on its genesis in the monotheistic speculations of Hesiod and Plato. He has also published on the mediaeval Latin philosophy of Thomas Aquinas and his commentatorial tradition, which includes John Poinsot ("John of St. Thomas"), from whom we may trace a foundational doctrine of signs for the interdisciplinary field of semiotics. Morrissey's current research explores how Eric Voegelin's philosophical studies of the historical processes of symbolization complement the pioneering interdisciplinary work by the semiotician and linguist Thomas Albert Sebeok towards a global semiotics.